Elizabeth Barrett Browning

Selected Verse

Elizabeth Barrett Browning
Browning
Selected Verse

Edited by
Johanna Brownell

CASTLE BOOKS

This edition published by
CASTLE BOOKS
a division of Book Sales, Inc.
114 Northfield Avenue
Edison, NJ 08837

Designed by Tony Meisel
Printed in the United States of America

ISBN 0-7858-1338-1

Contents

Introduction

Elizabeth Barrett Moulton-Barrett was born in Durham, England in 1806, the eldest of eleven children, whose father had made his fortune from his family's sugar plantation and estate in Jamaica. Largely self-educated, Elizabeth Barrett Moulton-Barrett began reading and writing verse before she was eight years old. Her love and fascination for the written word led her from a very early age to read the works of Shakespeare, Milton, Pope and Homer, as well as to learn Greek and Latin. By the age of thirteen, she had written her first work, on the *Battle of Marathon*, an epic in four volumes that her father had privately published. Elizabeth was an active child and spent a lot of time outdoors until an unfortunate riding accident at the age of fifteen. As she attempted to saddle her horse unaided, she injured her spine, an injury which kept her practically housebound for many years; seven years later, a blood vessel burst in her chest, which left her with a chronic cough. The effects of these injuries lasted until the end of her life. In her confinement, Elizabeth honed her poetic talents and, as she nursed her ailments, she found her true voice and calling as a poet. In 1832, Mr. Moulton-Barrett was forced to sell his country estate as a result of financial losses incurred in Jamaica, where he had made his fortune, and the consequent abolishment of slavery in the British isles. Elizabeth moved along with her family, first to Sidmouth in Devonshire, and then to Wimpole Street in London.

In 1838 Elizabeth Barrett published her first major work, *The Seraphim and Other Poems*, for which she received critical acclaim. In 1844, two volumes of her poetry appeared which set the tone for her critical and popular success as one of the great poets of the Victorian age. As a result, she found an admirer in the person of Robert Browning, himself an acclaimed poet, who wrote to her in praise of her work and talent. They exchanged letters for several months before meeting. By the time of their meeting, it was apparent that the two had fallen deeply in love and, in 1846, Elizabeth Barrett Moulton-Barrett married Robert Browning. The period of their courtship and betrothal is beautifully captured in *Sonnets from the Portuguese*, which were published in 1850. They moved to Italy, which was thought to be a better climate for Mrs. Browning's physical condition. Indeed, the Italian climate seemed to help her condition and, in 1849, Elizabeth Barrett Browning gave birth to a son,

Robert Wiedemann Barrett Browning. Notwithstanding several trips to England and France, the Brownings remained primarily in Florence until the death of Elizabeth Barrett Browning in 1861.

Although widely known for her sonnets and romantic verse, Elizabeth Barrett Browning was acutely aware of all that social and political issues going on around her. She railed against slavery and child labour in poems such as 'The Runaway Slave of Pilgrim's Point' and 'The Cry of the Children.' In addition, she became a sympathetic mouthpiece for Italian independence. Her epic work, *Aurora Leigh*, is both semi-autobiographical in nature, as well as it is socialistic in its purpose. Ultimately, though, it is her use of beautiful, illustrative imagery combined with her sensitivity to all people and creatures around her that elevate her work to greatness and categorize her as one of the great feminine voices in 19th century poetry, if not of all time.

From
The Seraphim, and Other Poems

Bereavement

WHEN some Beloveds, 'neath whose eyelids lay
The sweet lights of my childhood, one by one
Did leave me dark before the natural sun,
And I astonied fell and could not pray, –
A thought within me to myself did say,
'Is God less God that *thou* art left undone?
Rise, worship, bless Him, in this sackcloth spun,
As in that purple!' – But I answered Nay!
What child in his filial heart in words can loose
If he behold his tender father raise
The hands that chasten sorely? Can he choose
But sob in silence with an upward gaze? –
And *my* great Father, thinking fit to bruise,
Discerns in speechless tears both prayer and praise.

Consolation

ALL are not taken; there are left behind
Living Beloveds, tender looks to bring
And make the daylight still a happy thing,
And tender voices, to make soft the wind:
But if it were not so – if I could find
No love in all the world for comforting,
Nor any path but hollowly did ring
Where 'dust to dust' the love from life disjoined,
And if, before those sepulchres unmoving
I stood alone, (as some forsaken lamb
Goes bleating up the moors in weary dearth,)
Crying 'Where are ye, O my loved and loving?' –
I know a Voice would sound, 'Daughter, I AM.
Can I suffice for HEAVEN and not for earth?'

The Deserted Garden

I MIND me in the days departed,
How often underneath the sun
With childish bounds I used to run
    To a garden long deserted.

The beds and walks were vanished quite;
And wheresoe'er had struck the spade,
The greenest grasses Nature laid
    To sanctify her right.

I called the place my wilderness,
For no one entered there but I;
The sheep looked in, the grass to espy,
    And passed it ne'ertheless.

The trees were interwoven wild,
And spread their boughs enough about
To keep both sheep and shepherd out,
    But not a happy child.

Adventurous joy it was for me!
I crept beneath the boughs, and found
A circle smooth of mossy ground
    Beneath a poplar tree.

Old garden rose-trees hedged it in,
Bedropt with roses waxen-white
Well satisfied with dew and light
    And careless to be seen.

Long years ago it might befall,
When all the garden flowers were trim,
The grave old gardener prided him
    On these the most of all.

Some lady, stately overmuch,
Here moving with a silken noise,
Has blushed beside them at the voice
    That likened her to such.

And these, to make a diadem,
She often may have plucked and twined,
Half-smiling as it came to mind
    That few would look at *them*.

Oh, little thought that lady proud,
A child would watch her fair white rose,
When buried lay her whiter brows,
    And silk was changed for shroud!

Nor thought that gardener, (full of scorns
For men unlearned and simple phrase,)
A child would bring it all its praise
    By creeping through the thorns!

To me upon my low moss seat,
Though never a dream the roses sent
Of science or love's compliment,
    I ween they smelt as sweet.

It did not move my grief to see
The trace of human step departed:
Because the garden was deserted,
    The blither place for me!

Friends, blame me not! a narrow ken
Has childhood 'twixt the sun and sward;
We draw the moral afterward,
    We feel the gladness then.

And gladdest hours for me did glide
In silence at the rose-tree wall:
A thrush made gladness musical
    Upon the other side.

Nor he nor I did e'er incline
To peck or pluck the blossoms white;
How should I know but roses might
    Lead lives as glad as mine?

To make my hermit-home complete,
I brought dear water from the spring
Praised in its own low murmuring,
  And cresses glossy wet.

And so, I thought, my likeness grew
(Without the melancholy tale)
To 'gentle hermit of the dale,'
  And Angelina too.

For oft I read within my nook
Such minstrel stories; till the breeze
Made sounds poetic in the trees,
  And then I shut the book.

If I shut this wherein I write
I hear no more the wind athwart
Those trees, nor feel that childish heart
  Delighting in delight.

My childhood from my life is parted,
My footstep from the moss which drew
Its fairy circle round: anew
  The garden is deserted.

Another thrush may there rehearse
The madrigals which sweetest are;
No more for me! myself afar
  Do sing a sadder verse.

Ah me, ah me! when erst I lay
In that child's-nest so greenly wrought,
I laughed unto myself and thought
  'The time will pass away.'

And still I laughed, and did not fear
But that, whene'er was past away
The childish time, some happier play
  My womanhood would cheer.

I knew the time would pass away,
And yet, beside the rose-tree wall,
Dear God, how seldom, if at all,
 Did I look up to pray!

The time is past; and now that grows
The cypress high among the trees,
And I behold white sepulchres
 As well as the white rose,

When graver, meeker thoughts are given,
And I have learnt to lift my face,
Reminded how earth's greenest place
 The color draws from heaven,

It something saith for earthly pain,
But more for Heavenly promise free,
That I who was, would shrink to be
 That happy child again.

Man and Nature

A SAD man on a summer day
Did look upon the earth and say –

'Purple cloud the hill-top binding;
Folded hills the valleys wind in;
Valleys with fresh streams among you;
Streams with bosky trees along you;
Trees with many birds and blossoms;
Birds with music-trembling bosoms;
Blossoms dropping dews that wreathe you
To your fellow flowers beneath you;
Flowers that constellate on earth;
Earth that shakest to the mirth
Of the merry Titan Ocean,
All his shining hair in motion!
Why am I thus the only one
Who can be dark beneath the sun?'

But when the summer day was past,
He looked to heaven and smiled at last,
Self-answered so –

   'Because, O cloud,
Pressing with thy crumpled shroud
Heavily on mountain top, –
Hills that almost seem to drop
Stricken with a misty death
To the valleys underneath, –
Valleys sighing with the torrent, –
Waters streaked with branches horrent, –
Branchless trees that shake your head
Wildly o'er your blossoms spread
Where the common flowers are found, –
Flowers with foreheads to the ground, –
Ground that shriekest while the sea
With his iron smiteth thee –
I am, besides, the only one
Who can be bright *without* the sun.'

Memory and Hope

I.

BACK–LOOKING Memory
And prophet Hope both sprang from out the ground;
One, where flashing of cherubic sword
    Fell sad in Eden's ward,
And one, from Eden earth within the sound
Of the four rivers lapsing pleasantly,
What time the promise after curse was said,
    'Thy seed shall bruise his head.'

II.

Poor Memory's brain is wild,
As moonstruck by that flaming atmosphere
When she was born; her deep eyes shine and shone
    With light that conquereth sun
And stars to wanner paleness year by year:
With odorous gums she mixeth things defiled,
She trampleth down earth's grasses green and sweet
    With her far-wandering feet.

III.

She plucketh many flowers,
Their beauty on her bosom's coldness killing;
He teacheth every melancholy sound
    To wind and waters round;
She dropeth tears with seed where man is tilling
The rugged soil in his exhausted hours;
She smileth – ah me! In her smile doth go
    A mood of deeper woe.

IV.

Hope tripped out of sight,
Crowned with an Eden wreath she saw not wither,
And went a-nodding through the wilderness

With brow that shone no less
Than a sea-gull's wing, brought nearer by rough
    weather,
Searching the treeless rock for fruits of light;
Her fair quick feet being armed from stones and cold
    By slippers of pure gold.

V.

Memory did Hope much wrong
And, while she dreamed, her slippers stole away;
But still she wended on with mirth unheeding,
    Although her feet were bleeding,
Till Memory tracked her on a certain day,
And with most evil eyes did search her long
And cruelly, whereat she sank to ground
    In a stark deadly swound.

VI.

And so my Hope were slain,
Had it not been that THOU wast standing near –
Oh Thou who saidest 'Live,' to creatures lying
    In their own blood and dying!
For Thou her foreheard to thine heart didst rear
And make its silent pulses sing again,
Pouring a new light o'er her darkened eyne
    With tender tears from thine.

VII.

Therefore my Hope arose
From out her swound and gazed upon thy face,
And, meeting there that soft subduing look
    Which Peter's spirit shook,
Sank downward in a rapture to embrace
Thy pierced hands and feet with kisses close,
And prayed Thee to assist her evermore
    To 'reach the things before.'

A Sea-Side Walk

WE walked beside the sea,
After a day which perished silently
Of its own glory – like the princess weird
Who, combating the Genius, scorched and seared,
Uttered with burning breath, 'Ho! victory!'
And sank adown, an heap of ashes pale:
    So runs the Arab tale.

The sky above us showed
An universal and unmoving cloud,
On which, the cliffs permitted us to see
Only the outline of their majesty,
As master-minds, when gazed at by the crowd:
And, shining with a gloom, the water grey
    Swang in its moon-taught way.

Nor moon nor stars were out;
They did not dare to tread so soon about,
Though trembling, in the footsteps of the sun:
The light was neither night's nor day's, but one
Which, life-like, had a beauty in its doubt;
And Silence's impassioned breathings round
    Seemed wandering into sound.

O solemn-beating heart
Of nature! I have knowledge that thou art
Bound unto man's by cords he cannot sever;
And, what time they are slackened by him ever,
So to attest his own supernal part,
Still runneth thy vibration fast and strong,
    The slackened cord along:

For though we never spoke
Of the grey water and the shaded rock, –
Dark wave and stone unconsciously were fused
Into the plaintive speaking that we used,
Of absent friends and memories unforsook;
And, had we seen each other's face, we had
    Seen haply each was sad.

The Soul's Travelling

I.

I DWELL amid the city ever.
The great humanity which beats
Its life along the stony streets,
Like a strong and unsunned river
In a self-made course,
I sit and hearken while it rolls.
Very sad and very hoarse
Certes is the flow of souls;
Infinitest tendencies
By the finite prest and pent,
In the finite, turbulent:
How we tremble in surprise
When sometimes, with an awful sound,
God's great plummet strikes the ground!

II.

The champ of the steeds on the silver bit,
As they whirl the rich man's carriage by;
The beggar's whine as he looks at it, –
But it goes to fast for charity;
The trail on the street of the poor man's broom,
That the lady who walks to her palace-home,
On her silken skirt may catch no dust;
The tread of the business-men who must
Count their per-cents by the paces they take;
The cry of the babe unheard of its mother
Though it lie of her breast, while she thinks of her
    other
Laid yesterday where it will not wake;
The flower-girl's prayer to buy roses and pinks
Held out in the smoke, like stars by day;
The gin-door's oath that hollowly chinks
Guilt upon grief and wrong upon hate;
The cabman's cry to get out of the way;
The dustman's call down at the area-grate;

The young maid's jest, and the old wife's scold,
The haggling talk of the boys at a stall,
The fight in the street which is backed for gold,
The plea of the lawyers in Westminster Hall;
The drop on the stones of the blind man's staff
As he trades in his own grief's sacredness,
The brothel shriek, and the Newgate laugh,
The hum upon 'Change, and the organ's grinding,
(The grinder's face being nevertheless
Dry and vacant of even woe
While the children's hearts are leaping so
At the merry music's winding;)
The black-plumed funeral's creeping train,
Long and slow (and yet they will go
As fast as Life though it hurry and strain!)
Creeping the populous houses through
And nodding their plumes at either side, –
At many house, where an infant, new
To the sunshiny world, has just struggled and cried, –
At many a house where sitteth a bride
Trying to-morrow's coronals
With a scarlet blush to-day:
   Slowly creep the funerals,
As none should hear the noise and say
'The living, the living must go away
     To multiply the dead.'
   Hark! An upward shout is sent,
In grave strong joy from tower to steeple
     The bells ring out,
The trumpets sound, the people shout,
The young queen goes to her Parliament.
She turneth round her large blue eyes
More bright with childish memories
Than royal hopes, upon the people;
On either side she bows her head
   Lowly, with a queenly grace
And smile most trusting-innocent,
As if she smiled upon her mother;
The thousands press before each other
     To bless her to her face;
And booms the deep majestic voice

Through trump and drum, – 'May the queen rejoice
  In the people's liberties!'

III.

I dwell amid the city,
And hear the flow of souls in act and speech,
For pomp or trade, for merrymake or folly:
I hear the confluence and sum of each,
  And that is melancholy!
Thy voice is a complaint, O crowned city,
The blue sky covering thee like God's great pity.

IV.

O blue sky! It mindeth me
Of places where I used to see
Its vast unbroken circle thrown
From the far pale-peaked hill
Out to the last verge of ocean,
As by God's arm it were done
Then for the first time, with the emotion
Of that first impulse on it still.
Oh, we spirits fly at will
Faster than the winged steed
Whereof in old book we read,
With the sunlight foaming back
From his flanks to a misty wrack,
And his nostril reddening proud
As he breasteth the steep thunder-cloud, –
Smoother than Sabrina's chair
Gliding up from wave to air,
While she smileth debonair
Yet holy, coldly and yet brightly,
Like her own mooned waters nightly,
  Through her dripping hair.

V.

Very fast and smooth we fly,
Spirits, though the flesh be by;

All looks feed not from the eye
Nor all hearings from the ear:
We can hearken and espy
Without either, we can journey
Bold and gay as knight to tourney,
And, though we wear no visor down
To dark our countenance, the foe
Shall never chafe us as we go.

VI.

I am gone from peopled town!
It passeth its street-thunder round
My body which yet hears no sound,
For now another sound, another
Vision, my soul's senses have –
O'er a hundred valleys deep
Where the hills' green shadows sleep
Scarce known because the valley-trees
Cross those upland images,
O'er a hundred hills each other
Watching to the western wave,
I have travelled, – I have found
The silent, lone, remembered ground.

VII.

I have found a grassy niche
Hollowed in a seaside hill,
As if the ocean-grandeur which
Is aspectable from the place,
Had struck the hill as with a mace
Sudden and cleaving. You might fill
That little nook with the little cloud
Which sometimes lieth by the moon
To beautify a night of June;
A cavelike nook which, opening all
To the wide sea, is disallowed
From its own earth's sweet pastoral:
Cavelike, but roofless overheard
And made of verdant banks instead

Of any rock, with flowerets spread
Instead of spar and stalactite,
Cowslips and daisies gold and white:
Such pretty flowers on such green sward,
You think the sea they look toward
Doth serve them for another sky
As warm and blue as that on high.

VIII.

And in this hollow is a seat,
And when you shall have crept to it,
Slipping down the banks too steep
To be o'erbrowsed by the sheep,
Do not think – though at your feet
The cliff's disrupt – you shall behold
The line where earth and ocean meet;
You sit too much above to view
The solemn confluence of the two:
You can hear them as they greet,
You can hear that evermore
Distance-softened noise more old
Than Nereid's singing, the tide spent
Joining soft issues with the shore
In harmony of discontent,
And when you hearken to the grave
Lamenting of the underwave,
You must believe in earth's communion
Albeit you witness not the union.

IX.

Except that sound, the place is full
Of silences, which when you cull
By any word, it thrills you so
That presently you let them grow
To mediation's fullest length
Across your soul with a soul's strength:
And as they touch your soul, they borrow
Both of its grandeur and its sorrow,
That deathly odor which the clay

Leaves on its deathlessness alway.

X.

Alway! alway? must this be?
Rapid Soul from city gone,
Dost thou carry inwardly
What doth make the city's moan?
Must this deep sigh of thine own
Haunt thee with humanity?
Green visioned banks that are too steep
To be o'erbrowsed by the sheep,
May all sad thoughts adown you creep
Without a shepherd? Might sea,
Can we dwarf thy magnitude
And fit it to our straitest mood?
O fair, fair Nature, are we thus
Impotent and querulous
Among thy workings glorious,
Wealth and sanctities, that still
Leave us vacant and defiled
And wailing like a soft-kissed child,
Kissed soft against his will?

XI.

God, God!
With a child's voice I cry,
Weak, sad, confidingly –
God, God!
Though knowest eyelids, raised not always up
Unto thy love, (as none of ours are) droop
    As ours, o'er many a tear;
Thou knowest, though thy universe is broad,
Two little tears suffice to cover all:
Thou knowest, Thou who art so prodigal
Of beauty, we are oft nut stricken deer
Expiring in the woods, that care for none
Of those delightsome flowers they die upon.

XII.

O blissful Month which breathed the mournful breath
We name our souls self-spoilt! – by that strong passion
Which paled Thee once with sighs, by that strong death
Which made Thee once unbreathing – from the wrack
Themselves have called around them, call them back,
Back to Thee in continuous aspiration!
　　For here, O Lord,
Foe here they travel vainly, vainly pass
From city-pavement to untrodden sward
Where the lark finds her deep nest in the grass
Cold with the earth's last dew. Yea, very vain
The greatest speed of all these souls of men
Unless they travel upward to the throne
Where sittest THOU the satisfying ONE,
With help for sins and holy perfectings
For all requirements: while the archangel, raising
Unto thy face his full ecstatic gazing,
Forgets the rush and rapture of his wings.

Stanzas

I MAY sing; but minstrel's singing
Ever ceaseth with his playing.
I may smile; but time is bringing
Thoughts for smiles to wear away in.
I may view thee, mutely loving;
But *shall* view thee so in dying!
I may sigh; but life's removing,
And with breathing endeth sighing!
                        Be it so!

When no song of mine comes near thee,
Will its memory fail to soften?
When no smile of mine can cheer thee,
Will thy smile be used as often?
When my looks the darkness boundeth,
Will thine own be lighted after?
When my sigh no longer soundeth,
Will thou list another's laughter?
                        Be it so!

A Supplication for Love

HYMN I

'The Lord Jesus, although gone to the Father, and we see Him no more, is still present with His Church; and in His heavenly glory expends upon her as intense a love, as in the agony of the garden, and the crucifixion of the tree. Those eyes that wept, still gaze upon her.'

> *— Recalled words of an extempore Discourse,*
> *preached at Sidmouth, 1833.*

GOD, named Love, whose fount thou art,
    Thy crownless Church before Thee stands,
With too much hating in her heart,
    And too much striving in her hands!

O loving Lord! O slain for love!
    Thy blood upon thy garments came –
Inwrap their folds our brows above,
    Before we tell Thee all our shame!

'Love and I loved you,' was the sound
    That on my lips expiring sate!
Sweet words, in bitter strivings drowned!
    We hated as the worldly hate.

The spear that pierced for love thy side
    We dared for wrathful use to crave;
And with our cruel noise denied
    Its silence to thy blood-red grave!

Ah, blood! That speaketh more of love
    Than Abel's – could we speak like Cain,
And grieve and scare that holy Dove,
    The parting love-gift of the Slain?

Yet, Lord, thy wronged love fulfil!
    Thy Church, though fallen, before Thee stands —
Behold, the voice is Jacob's still,
    Albeit the hands are Esau's hands!

Hast Thou no tears, like those besprent
    Upon thy Zion's ancient part?
No moving looks, like those which sent
    Their softness through a traitor's heart?

No touching tale of anguish dear;
    Whereby like children we may creep,
All trembling, to each other near,
    And view each other's face and weep?

Oh, move us — THOU hast power to move —
    One in the one Beloved to be!
Teach us the heights and depths of love —
    Give THINE — that we may love like THEE!

The Mediator

Hymn II

'As greatest of all sacrifices was required, we may be assured that no other would have sufficed.'

— Boyd's *Essay on the Atonement.*

HOW high Thou art! Our songs can own
  No music Thou couldst stoop to hear!
But still the Son's expiring groan
  Is vocal in the Father's ear.

How pure Thou art! Our hands are dyed
  With curses, red with murder's hue –
But HE hath stretched HIS hands to hide
  The sins that pierced them from thy view.

How strong Thou art! We tremble lest
  The thunders of thine arm be moved –
But HE is lying on thy breast,
  And Thou must clasp they best Beloved!

How kind Thou art! Thou didst not choose
  To joy in Him for ever so;
But that embrace Thou wilt not loose
  For vengeance, didst for love forego!

High God, and pure, and strong, and kind
  The low, the foul, the feeble spare!
Thy brightness in his face we find –
  Behold our darkness only *there*!

The Weeping Saviour

Hymn III

'Whether his countenance can thee affright,
Tears in his eyes quench the amazing light.'
– Donne.

WHEN Jesus' friend had ceased to be,
    Still Jesus' heart its friendship kept –
'Where have ye laid him?' – 'Come and see!'
    But ere his eyes could see, they wept.

Lord! Not in sepulchres alone
    Corruption's worm is rank and free:
The shroud of death our bosom's own –
    The shades of sorrow! Come and see!

Come, Lord! God's image cannot shine
    Where sin's funereal darkness lowers –
Come! Turn those weeping eyes of thine
    Upon those sinning souls of ours!

And let those eyes with shepherd care
    Their moving watch above us keep;
Till love the strength of sorrow wear,
    And, as Thou weepedst, *we* may weep!

For surely we may weep to know,
    So dark and deep our spirits' stain;
That, had thy blood refused to flow
    Thy very tears had flowed in vain.

The Measure

HYMN IV

'He comprehended the dust of the earth in a measure'
— *Isaiah* xl.

'Thou givest them tears to drink in a measure'
— *Psalm* lxxx.

I.

GOD the Creator, with a pulseless hand
Of unoriginated power, hath weighed
The dust and earth tears of man in one
    Measure, and by one weight:
    So saith his holy book.

II.

Shall we, then, who have issued from the dust
And there return — shall we, who toil for the dust,
And wrap our winnings in this dusty life,
    Say 'No more tears, Lord God!
    The measure runneth o'er'?

III.

Oh, Holder of the balance, laughest Thou?
Nay, Lord! be gentler to our foolishness,
For his sake who assumed our dust and turns
    On Thee pathetic eyes
    still moistened with our tears.

IV.

And teach us, O our Father, while we weep,
To look in patience upon earth and learn –
Waiting, in that meek gesture, till at last
    These tearful eyes be filled
    With the dry dust of death.

The Young Queen

'This awful responsibility is imposed upon me so suddenly and at so early a period of my life, that I should feel myself utterly oppressed by the burden, were I not sustained by the hope that Divine Providence, which has called me to this work, will give me strength for the performance of it.'

— The Queen's Declaration in Council.

I.

The shroud is yet unspread
To wrap our crownèd dead;
His soul hath scarcely hearkened for the thrilling word of doom;
And Death, that makes serene
Ev'n brows where crowns have been,
Hath scarcely time to meeten his for silence of the tomb.

II.

St. Paul's king-dirging note
The city's heart hath smote –
The city's heart is struck with thought more solemn than the tone!
A shadow sweeps apace
Before the nation's face,
Confusing in a shapeless blot the sepulchre and throne.

III.

The palace sounds with wail –
The courtly dames are pale –
A widow o'er the purple bows, and weeps its splendor dim:
And we who hold the boon,
A king for freedom won,
Do feel eternity rise up between our thanks and him.

IV.

And while all things express
    All glory's nothingness,
A royal maiden treadeth firm where that departed trod!
    The deathly scented crown
    Weighs her shining ringlets down;
But calm she lifts her trusting face, and calleth upon God.

V.

Her thoughts are deep within her:
    No outward pageants win her
From memories that in her soul are rolling wave on wave –
    Her palace walls enring
    The dust that was a king –
And very cold beneath her feet, she feels her father's grave.

VI.

And One, as fair as she,
    Can scarce forgotten be, –
Who clasped a little infant dead, for all a kingdom's worth!
    The mourned, blessed One,
    Who views Jehovah's throne,
Aye smiling to the angels, that she lost a throne on earth.

VII.

Perhaps our youthful Queen
    Remembers what has been –
Her childhood's rest by loving heart, and sport on grassy sod –
    Alas! can other's wear
    A mother's heart for her?
But calm she lifts her trusting face, and calleth upon God.

VIII.

Yea! call on God, thou maiden
  Of spirit nobly laden,
And leave such happy days behind, for happy-making years!
  A nation looks to thee
  For steadfast sympathy:
Make room within thy bright clear eyes for all its gathered tears.

IX.

And so the grateful isles
  Shall give thee back their smiles,
And as thy mother joys in thee, in them shalt *thou* rejoice;
  Rejoice to meekly bow
  A somewhat paler brow,
While the King of kings shall bless thee by the British people's
  voice!

From
Poems of 1844

Adequacy

NOW, by the verdure on thy thousand hills,
Beloved England, doth the earth appear
Quite good enough for men to overbear
The will of God in, with rebellious wills!
We cannot say the morning-sun fulfils
Ingloriously its course, nor that the clear
Strong stars without significance insphere
Our habitation: we, meantime, our ills
Heap up against this good and lift a cry
Against this work-day world, this ill-spread feast,
As if ourselves were better certainly
Than what we come to. Maker and High Priest,
I ask thee not my joys to multiply, –
Only to make me worthier of the least.

An Apprehension

IF all the gentlest-hearted friends I know
Concentred in one heart their gentleness,
That still grew gentler till its pulse was less
For life than pity, – I should yet be slow
To bring my own heart nakedly below
The palm of such a friend, that he should press
Motive, condition, means, appliances,
My false ideal joy and fickle woe,
Out full to light and knowledge; I should fear
Some plait between the brows, some rougher chime
In the free voice. O angels, let your flood
Of bitter scorn dash on me! do ye hear
What *I* say who hear calmly all the time
This everlasting face to face with GOD?

Cheerfulness Taught By Reason

I THINK we are too ready with complaint
In this fair world of God's. Had we no hope
Indeed beyond the zenith and the slope
Of yon gray blank of sky, we might grow faint
To muse upon eternity's constraint
Round our aspirant souls; but since the scope
Must widen early, is it well to droop,
For a few days consumed in loss and taint?
O pusillanimous Heart, be comforted
And, like a cheerful traveller, take the road
Singing beside the hedge. What if the bread
Be bitter in thine inn, and thou unshod
To meet the flints? At least it may be said
'Because the way is *short*, I thank thee, God.'

Comfort

SPEAK low to me, my Saviour, low and sweet
From out the hallelujahs, sweet and low
Lest I should fear and fall, and miss Thee so
Who art not missed by any that entreat.
Speak to me as to Mary at thy feet!
And if no precious gums my hands bestow,
Let my tears drop like amber while I go
In reach of thy divinest voice complete
In humanest affection – thus, in sooth,
To lose the sense of losing. As a child,
Whose song-bird seeks the wood for evermore
Is sung to in its stead by mother's mouth
Till, sinking on her breast, love-reconciled,
He sleeps the faster that he wept before.

Discontent

LIGHT human nature is too lightly tost
And ruffled without cause, complaining on –
Restless with rest, until, being overthrown,
It learneth to lie quiet. Let a frost
Or a small wasp have crept to the inner-most
Of our ripe peach, or let the wilful sun
Shine westward of our window, – straight we run
A furlong's sigh as if the world were lost.
But what time through the heart and through the brain
God hath transfixed us, – we, so moved before,
Attain to a calm. Ay, shouldering weights of pain,
We anchor in deep waters, safe from shore,
And hear submissive o'er the stormy main
God's chartered judgments walk for evermore.

Exaggeration

WE overstate the ills of life, and take
Imagination (given us to bring down
The choirs of singing angels overshone
By God's clear glory) down our earth to rake
The dismal snows instead, flake following flake,
To cover all the corn; we walk upon
The shadow of hills across a level thrown,
And pant like climbers: near the alder brake
We sigh so loud, the nightingale within
Refuses to sing loud, as else she would.
O brothers, let us leave the shame and sin
Of taking vainly, in a plaintive mood,
The holy name of GRIEF! – holy herein
That by the grief of ONE came all our good.

Futurity

AND, O beloved voices, upon which
Ours passionately call because erelong
Ye brake off in the middle of that song
We sang together softly, to enrich
The poor world with the sense of love, and witch,
The heart out of things evil, – I am strong,
Knowing ye are not lost for aye among
The hills, with last year's thrush. God keeps a niche
In Heaven to hold our idols; and albeit
He brake them to our faces and denied
That our close kisses should impair their white,
I know we shall behold them raised, complete,
The dust swept from their beauty, – glorified
New Memnons singing in the great God-light.

Grief

I TELL you, hopeless grief is passionless;
That only men incredulous of despair,
Half-taught in anguish, through the midnight air
Beat upward to God's throne in loud access
Of shrieking and reproach. Full desertness,
In souls as countries, lieth silent-bare
Under the blanching, vertical eye-glare
Of the absolute Heavens. Deep-hearted man, express
Grief for thy Dead in silence like to death –
Most like a monumental statue set
In everlasting watch and moveless woe
Till itself crumble to the dust beneath.
Touch it; the marble eyelids are not wet:
If it could weep, it could arise and go.

Insufficiency

WHEN I attain to utter forth in verse
Some inward thought, my soul throbs audibly
Along my pulses, yearning to be free
And something farther, fuller, higher, rehearse
To the individual, true, and the universe,
In consummation of right harmony:
But, like a wind-exposed distorted tree,
We are blown against for ever by the curse
Which breathes through Nature.Oh, the world is weak!
The effluence of each is false to all,
And what we best conceive we fail to speak.
Wait, soul, until thine ashen garments fall,
And then resume thy broken strains, and seek
Fit peroration without let or thrall.

Irreparableness

I HAVE been in the meadows all the day
And gathered there the nosegay that you see
Singing within myself as bird or bee
When such do field-work on a morn of May.
But, now I look upon my flowers, decay
Has met them in my hands more fatally
Because more warmly clasped, – and sobs are free
To come instead of songs. What do you say,
Sweet counsellors, dear friends? that I should go
Back straightway to the fields and gather more?
Another, sooth, may do it, but not I!
My heart is very tired, my strength is low,
My hands are full of blossoms plucked before,
Held dead within them till myself shall die.

The Look

THE Saviour looked on Peter. Ay, no word,
No gesture of reproach; the Heavens serene
Though heavy with armed justice, did not lean
Their thunders that way: the forsaken Lord
Looked only, on the traitor. None record
What that look was, none guess; for those who have
    seen
Wronged lovers loving through a death-pang keen,
Or pale-cheeked martyrs smiling to a sword,
Have missed Jehovah at the judgment-call.
And Peter, from the height of blasphemy –
'I never knew this man' – did quail and fall
As knowing straight THAT GOD; and turned free
And went out speechless from the face of all
And filled the silence, weeping bitterly.

The Meaning of the Look

I THINK that look of Christ might seem to say –
'Thou Peter! art thou then a common stone
Which I at last must break my heart upon
For all God's charge to his high angels may
Guard my foot better? Did I yesterday
Wash *thy* feet, my beloved, that they should run
Quick to deny me 'neath the morning sun?
And do thy kisses, like the rest, betray?
The cock crows coldly. – Go, and manifest
A late contrition, but no bootless fear!
For when thy final need is dreariest,
Thou shalt not be denied, as I am here;
My voice to God and angels shall attest,
Because I KNOW *this man, let him be clear.'*

On a Portrait of Wordsworth
by B. R. Haydon

First printed in the *Atheneum*, October 29, 1842, as
'On Mr. Haydon's Portrait of Wordsworth.'

WORDSWORTH upon Helvellyn! Let the cloud
Ebb audibly along the mountain-wind,
Then break against the rock, and show behind
The lowland valleys floating up to crowd
The sense with beauty. He with forehead bowed
And humble-lidded eyes, as one inclined
Before the sovran thought of his own mind,
And very meek with inspirations proud,
Takes here his rightful place as poet-priest
By the high altar, singing prayer and prayer
To the higher Heavens. A noble vision free
Our Haydon's hand has flung out from the mist:
No portrait this, with Academic air!
This is the poet and his poetry.

Pain in Pleasure

A THOUGHT ay like a flower upon mine heart,
And drew around it other thoughts like bees
For multitude and thirst of sweetnesses;
Whereat rejoicing, I desired the art
Of the Greek whistler, who to wharf and mart
Could lure those insect swarms from orange-trees
That I might hive with me such thoughts and please
My soul so, always. Foolish counterpart
Of a weak man's vain wishes! While I spoke,
The thought I called a flower grew nettle-rough
The thoughts, called bees, stung me to festering:
Oh, entertain (cried Reason as she woke)
Your best and gladdest thoughts but long enough,
And they will all prove sad enough to sting!

Past and Future

MY future will not copy fair my past
On any leaf but Heaven's. Be fully done
Supernal Will! I would not fain be one
Who, satisfying thirst and breaking fast,
Upon the fulness of the heart at last
Says no grace after meat. My wine has run
Indeed out of my cup, and there is none
To gather up the bread of my repast
Scattered and trampled; yet I find some good
In earth's green herbs, and streams that bubble up
Clear from the darkling ground, – content until
I sit with angels before better food:
Dear Christ! when thy new vintage fills my cup,
This hand shall shake no more, nor that wine spill.

Patience Taught by Nature

'O DREARY life,' we cry, 'O dreary life!'
And still the generations of the birds
Sing through our sighing, and the flocks and herds
Serenely live while we are keeping strife
With Heaven's true purpose in us, as a knife
Against which we may struggle! Ocean girds
Unslackened the dry land, savannah-swards
Unweary sweep, hills watch unworn, and rife
Meek leaves drop yearly from the forest-trees
To show, above, the unwasted stars that pass
In their old glory: O thou God of old,
Grant me some smaller grace than comes to these! –
But so much patience as a blade of grass
Grows by, contented through the heat and cold.

Perplexed Music

AFFECTIONATELY INSCRIBED TO E. J.

EXPERIENCE, like a pale musician, holds
A dulcimer of patience in his hand,
Whence harmonies, we cannot understand,
Of God's will in his worlds, the strain unfolds
In sad-perplexed minors: deathly colds
Fall on us while we hear, and countermand
Our sanguine heart back from the fancyland
With nightingales in visionary wolds.
We murmur ' Where is any certain tune
Or measured music in such notes as these? '
But angels, leaning from the golden seat,
Are not so minded; their fine ear hath won
The issue of completed cadences,
And, smiling down the stars, they whisper – SWEET.

The Prisoner

I COUNT the dismal time by months and years
Since last I felt the green sward under foot,
And the great breath of all things summer-mute
Met mine upon my lips. Now earth appears
As strange to me as dreams of distant spheres
Or thoughts of Heaven we weep at. Nature's lute
Sounds on, behind this door so closely shut,
A strange wild music to the prisoner's ears,
Dilated by the distance, till the brain
Grows dim with fancies which it feels too fine:
While ever, with a visionary pain,
Past the precluded senses, sweep and shine
Streams, forests, glades, and many a golden train
Of sunlit hills transfigured to Divine.

The Seraph and Poet

THE seraph sings before the manifest
God-One, and in the burning of the Seven,
And with the full life of consummate Heaven
Heaving beneath him like a mother's breast
Warm with her first-born's slumber in that nest.
The poet sings upon the earth grave-riven,
Before the naughty world, soon self-forgiven
For wronging him, – and in the darkness prest
From his own soul by worldly weights. Even so,
Sing, seraph with the glory! heaven is high;
Sing, poet with the sorrow! earth is low:
The universe's inward voices cry
'Amen' to either song of joy and woe:
Sing, seraph, – poet, – sing on equally!

The Soul's Expression

WITH stammering lips and insufficient sound
I strive and struggle to deliver right
That music of my nature, day and night
With dream and thought and feeling interwound,
And only answering all the senses round
With octaves of a mystic depth and height
Which step out grandly to the infinite
From the dark edges of the sensual ground.
This song of soul I struggle to outbear
Through portals of the sense, sublime and whole,
And utter all myself into the air:
But if I did it, – as the thunder-roll
Breaks its own cloud, my flesh would perish there,
Before that dread apocalypse of soul.

Substitution

WHEN some beloved voice that was to you
Both sound and sweetness, faileth suddenly,
And silence, against which you dare not cry,
Aches round you like a strong disease and new —
What hope? what help? what music will undo
That silence to your sense? Not friendship's sigh,
Not reason's subtle count; not melody
Of viols, nor of pipes that Faunus blew;
Not songs of poets, nor of nightingales
Whose hearts leap upward through the cypress-trees
To the clear moon; nor yet the spheric laws
Self-chanted, nor the angels' sweet 'All hails,'
Met in the smile of God: nay, none of these.
Speak THOU, availing Christ! — and fill this pause.

Tears

THANK God, bless God, all ye who suffer not
More grief than ye can weep for. That is well –
That is light grieving! lighter, none befell
Since Adam forfeited the primal lot.
Tears! what are tears? The babe weeps in its cot,
The mother singing, at her marriage-bell
The bride weeps, and before the oracle
Of high-faned hills the poet has forgot
Such moisture on his cheeks. Thank God for grace,
Ye who weep only! If, as some have done,
Ye grope tear-blinded in a desert place
And touch but tombs, – look up! those tears will run
Soon in long rivers down the lifted face,
And leave the vision clear for stars and sun.

A Thought for a Lonely Death-Bed

INSCRIBED TO MY FRIEND E.C.

IF God compel thee to this destiny,
To die alone, with none beside thy bed
To ruffle round with sobs thy last word said
And mark with tears the pulses ebb from thee, –
Pray then alone, 'O Christ, come tenderly!
By thy forsaken Sonship in the red
Drear wine-press, – by the wilderness out-spread, –
And the lone garden where thine agony
Fell bloody from thy brow, – by all of those
Permitted desolations, comfort mine!
No earthly friend being near me, interpose
No deathly angel 'twixt my face and thine,
But stoop Thyself to gather my life's rose,
And smile away my mortal to Divine!'

The Two Sayings

TWO sayings of the Holy Scriptures beat
Like pulses in the Church's brow and breast;
And by them we find rest in our unrest
And, heart deep in salt-tears, do yet entreat
God's fellowship as if on heavenly seat.
The first is JESUS WEPT, – whereon is prest
Full many a sobbing face that drops its best
And sweetest waters on the record sweet:
And one is where the Christ, denied and scorned
LOOKED UPON PETER. Oh, to render plain
By help of having loved a little and mourned,
That look of sovran love and sovran pain
Which HE, who could not sin yet suffered, turned
On him who could reject but not sustain!

To George Sand

A Desire

THOU large-brained woman and large-hearted man,
Self-called George Sand! whose soul, amid the lions
Of thy tumultuous senses, moans defiance
And answers roar for roar, as spirits can:
I would some mild miraculous thunder ran
Above the applauded circus, in appliance
Of thine own nobler nature's strength and science,
Drawing two pinions, white as wings of swan,
From thy strong shoulders, to amaze the place
With holier light! that thou to woman's claim
And man's, mightst join beside the angel's grace
Of a pure genius sanctified from blame
Till child and maiden pressed to thine embrace
To kiss upon thy lips a stainless fame.

To George Sand

TRUE genius, but true woman! dost deny
The woman's nature with a manly scorn,
And break away the gauds and armlets worn
By weaker women in captivity?
Ah, vain denial! that revolted cry
Is sobbed in by a woman's voice forlorn, –
Thy woman's hair, my sister, all unshorn
Floats back dishevelled strength in agony
Disproving thy man's name: and while before
The world thou burnest in a poet-fire,
We see thy woman-heart beat evermore
Through the large flame. Beat purer, heart, and higher,
Till God unsex thee on the heavenly shore
Where unincarnate spirits purely aspire!

Work

WHAT are we set on earth for? Say, to toil;
Nor seek to leave thy tending of the vines
For all the heat o' the day, till it declines,
And Death's mild curfew shall from work assoil.
God did anoint thee with his odorous oil,
To wrestle, not to reign; and He assigns
All thy tears over, like pure crystallines,
For younger fellow-workers of the soil
To wear for amulets. So others shall
Take patience, labor, to their heart and hand
From thy hand and thy heart and thy brave cheer,
And God's grace fructify through thee to all.
The least flower with a brimming cup may stand,
And share its dew-drop with another near.

Work and Contemplation

THE woman singeth at her spinning-wheel
A pleasant chant, ballad or barcarole;
She thinketh of her song, upon the whole,
Far more than of her flax; and yet the reel
Is full, and artfully her fingers feel
With quick adjustment, provident control,
The lines – too subtly twisted to unroll –
Out to a perfect thread. I hence appeal
To the dear Christian Church – that we may do
Our Father's business in these temples mirk,
Thus swift and steadfast, thus intent and strong;
While thus, apart from toil, our souls pursue
Some high calm spheric tune, and prove our work
The better for the sweetness of our song.

A Child Asleep

First printed in Finden's *Tableaux* for 1840 as
'The Dream.'

I.

How he sleepeth, having drunken
    Weary childhood's mandragore!
From his pretty eyes have sunken
    Pleasures, to make room for more;
Sleeping near the withered nosegay which he pulled
    the day before.

II.

Nosegays! leave them for the waking;
    Throw them earthward where they grew.
Dim are such, beside the breaking
    Amaranths he looks unto:
Folded eyes see brighter colours than the open ever do.

III.

Heaven-flowers, rayed by shadows golden
    From the paths they sprang beneath,
Now perhaps divinely holden,
    Swing against him in a wreath:
We may think so from the quickening of his bloom and
    of his breath.

IV.

Vision unto vision calleth
    While the young child dreameth on:
Fair, O dreamer, thee befalleth
    With the glory thou hast won!
Darker wert thou in the garden, yestermorn, by
    summer sun.

V.

We should see the spirits ringing
    Round thee, – were the clouds away:
'T is the child-heart draws them, singing
    In the silent-seeming clay –
Singing! stars that seem the mutest go in music all the
    way.

VI.

As the moths around a taper,
    As the bees around a rose,
As the gnats around a vapour,
    So the Spirits group and close
Round about a holy childhood as if drinking its repose.

VII.

Shapes of brightness overlean thee,
    Flash their diadems of youth
On the ringlets which half screen thee,
    While thou smilest . . . not in sooth
Thy smile, but the overfair one, dropt from some
    ethereal mouth.

VIII.

Haply it is angels' duty,
    During slumber, shade by shade
To fine down this childish beauty
    To the thing it must be made,
Ere the world shall bring it praises, or the tomb shall
    see it fade.

IX.

Softly, softly! make no noises!
    Now he lieth dead and dumb;
Now he hears the angels' voices
    Folding silence in the room:

Now he muses deep the meaning of the Heaven-words
    as they come.

X.

Speak not! he is consecrated;
    Breathe no breath across his eyes:
Lifted up and separated,
    On the hand of God he lies
In a sweetness beyond touching, held in cloistral
    sanctities.

XI.

Could ye bless him, father – mother?
    Bless the dimple in his cheek?
Dare ye look at one another,
    And the benediction speak?
Would ye not break out in weeping and confess
    yourselves too weak?

XII.

He is harmless, ye are sinful;
    Ye are troubled, he at ease;
From his slumber, virtue winful
    Floweth outward with increase.
Dare not bless him! but be blessed by his peace, and go
    in peace.

Crowned and Wedded

Queen Victoria and Prince Albert of Saxe-Coburg –Gotha were betrothed in October 1839, and married February 1, 1840. This poem was first printed in the *Atheneum* for February 15, 1840, as 'The Crowned and Wedded Queen.'

I.

WHEN last before her people's face her own fair face she bent,
Within the meek projection of that shade she was content
To erase the child-smile from her lips, which seemed as if it might
Be still kept holy from the world to childhood still in sight –
To erase it with a solemn vow, a princely vow – to rule;
A priestly vow – to rule by grace of God the pitiful,
A very godlike vow – to rule in right and righteousness,
And with the law and for the land – so God the vower bless!

II.

The minster was alight that day, but not with fire, I ween;
And long-drawn glitterings swept adown that mighty aisled scene;
The priests stood stoled in their pomp, the sworded chiefs in
      theirs,
And so, the collared knights, and so, the civil ministers,
And so, the waiting lords and dames, and little pages best
At holding trains, and legates so, from countries east and west;
So, alien princes, native peers, and high-born ladies bright,
Along whose brows the Queen's, now crowned, flashed coronets
to light;
And so, the people at the gates with priestly hands on high,
Which bring the first anointing to all legal majesty;
And so the DEAD, who lie in rows beneath the minster floor,
There verily an awful state maintaining evermore;
The statesman whose clean palm will kiss no bribe, whate'er it be,
The courtier who for no fair queen will rise up to his knee,
The court-dame who for no court-tire will leave her shroud
      behind,
The laureate, who no courtlier rhyme than 'dust to dust' can find,

The kings and queens who having made that vow and worn that
    crown,
Descended unto lower thrones, and darker, deep adown:
Dieu et mon droit – what is't to them? what meaning can it have?
The King of kings, the right of death – God's judgment and the
    grave.
And when betwixt the quick and dead the young fair queen had
    vowed,
The living shouted, 'May she live! Victoria, live!' aloud:
And, as the loyal shouts went up, true spirits prayed between,
'The blessings happy monarchs have be thine, O crowned queen!'

III.

But now before her people's face she bendeth hers anew,
And calls them, while she vows, to be her witness thereunto.
She vowed to rule, and in that oath her childhood put away:
She doth maintain her womanhood, in vowing love today.
O lovely lady! let her vow! such lips become such vows,
And fairer goeth bridal wreath than crown with vernal brows.
O lovely lady! let her vow! yea, let her vow to love!
And though she be no less a queen, with purples hung above,
The pageant of a court behind, the royal kin around,
And woven gold to catch her looks turned maidenly to ground,
Yet may the bride-veil hide from her a little of that state,
While loving hopes for retinues about her sweetness wait.
She vows to love who vowed to rule – (the chosen at her side)
Let none say, God preserve the queen! but rather, Bless the bride!
None blow the trump, none bend the knee, none violate the
    dream
Wherein no monarch but a wife she to herself may seem.
Or if ye say, Preserve the queen! oh, breathe it inward low –
She is a *woman*, and *beloved*! and 't is enough but so.
Count it enough, thou noble prince, who tak'st her by the hand,
And claimest for thy lady-love, our lady of the land!
And since, Prince Albert, men have called thy spirit high and rare,
And true to truth and brave for truth, as some at Augsburg were,
We charge thee by thy lofty thoughts and by thy poet-mind,
Which not by glory and degree takes measure of mankind,
Esteem that wedded hand less dear for sceptre than for ring,
And hold her uncrowned womanhood to be the royal thing.

IV.

And now, upon our queen's last vow what blessings shall we pray?
None straitened to a shallow crown will suit our lips today:
Behold, they must be free as love, they must be broad as free,
Even to the borders of heaven's light and earth's humanity,
Long live she! – send up loyal shouts, and true hearts pray
 between, –
'The blessings happy PEASANTS have, be thine, O crowned queen!'

The Cry of the Children

'Alas, alas, why do you gaze at me with your eyes, my children.'
— *Medea.*

'The Cry of the Children,' first published in *Blackwood's Magazine,* for August, 1843, was called forth by Mr. Horne's report as assistant Commissioner on the employment of children in mines and factories.

I.

Do ye hear the children weeping, O my brothers,
    Ere the sorrow comes with years?
They are leaning their young heads against their
    mothers,
    And *that* cannot stop their tears.
The young lambs are bleating in the meadows,
    The young birds are chirping in the nest;
The young fawns are playing with the shadows,
    The young flowers are blowing toward the west —
But the young, young children, O my brothers,
    They are weeping bitterly!
They are weeping in the playtime of the others,
    In the country of the free.

II.

Do you question the young children in the sorrow,
    Why their tears are falling so?
The old man may weep for his to-morrow
    Which is lost in Long Ago;
The old tree is leafless in the forest,
    The old year is ending in the frost,
The old wound, if stricken, is the sorest,
    The old hope is hardest to be lost :
But the young, young children, O my brothers,
    Do you ask them why they stand
Weeping sore before the bosoms of their mothers,
    In our happy Fatherland?

III.

They look up with their pale and sunken faces,
    And their looks are sad to see,
For the man's grief abhorrent, draws and presses
    Down the cheeks of infancy;
'Your old earth,' they say, 'is very dreary;
    Our young feet,' they say, 'are very weak;
Few paces have we taken, yet are weary –
    Our grave-rest is very far to seek:
Ask the old why they weep, and not the children,
    For the outside earth is cold,
And we young ones stand without, in our bewildering,
    And the graves are for the old!

IV.

'True,' say the children, 'it may happen
    That we die before our time:
Little Alice died last year her grave is shapen
    Like a snowball, in the rime.
We looked into the pit prepared to take her:
    Was no room for any work in the close clay!
From the sleep wherein she lieth none will wake her,
    Crying, "Get up, little Alice! it is day."
If you listen by that grave, in sun and shower,
    With your ear down, little Alice never cries;
Could we see her face, be sure we should not know
her,
    For the smile has time for growing in her eyes:
And merry go her moments, lulled and stilled in
    The shroud, by the kirk-chime!
It is good when it happens,' say the children,
    'That we die before our time.'

V.

Alas, the wretched children! they are seeking
    Death in life, as best to have:
They are binding up their hearts away from breaking,
    With a cerement from the grave.

Go out, children, from the mine and from the city,
    Sing out, children, as the little thrushes do;
Pluck you handfuls of the meadow-cowslips pretty.
    Laugh aloud, to feel your fingers let them
    through!
But they answer, 'Are your cowslips of the meadows
    Like our weeds anear the mine?
Leave us quiet in the dark of the coal-shadows,
    From your pleasures fair and fine!

VI.

'For oh,' say the children, 'we are weary,
    And we cannot run or leap;
If we cared for any meadows, it were merely
    To drop down in them and sleep.
Our knees tremble sorely in the stooping,
    We fall upon our faces, trying to go;
And, underneath our heavy eyelids drooping
    The reddest flower would look as pale as snow.
For, all day, we drag our burden tiring
    Through the coal-dark, underground;
Or, all day, we drive the wheels of iron
    In the factories, round and round.

VII.

'For all day, the wheels are droning, turning;
    Their wind comes in our faces,
Till our hearts turn, our heads, with pulses burning,
    And the walls turn in their places:
Turns the sky in the high window blank and reeling,
    Turns the long light that droppeth down the wall,
Turn the black flies that crawl along the ceiling:
    All are turning, all the day, and we with all.
And all day, the iron wheels are droning,
    And sometimes we could pray,
"O ye wheels," (breaking out in a mad moaning)
    "Stop! be silent for to-day!"'

VIII.

Ay! be silent! Let them hear each other breathing
    For a moment, mouth to mouth!
Let them touch each other's hands, in a fresh wreathing
    Of their tender human youth!
Let them feel that this cold metallic motion
    Is not all the life God fashions or reveals:
Let them prove their inward souls against the notion
    That they live in you, or under you, O wheels!
Still, all day, the iron wheels go onward,
    Grinding life down from its mark;
And the children's souls, which God is calling sunward,
    Spin on blindly in the dark.

IX.

Now tell the poor young children, O my brothers,
    To look up to Him and pray;
So the blessed One, who blesseth all the others,
    Will bless them another day.
They answer, 'Who is God that He should hear us,
    While the rushing of the iron wheels is stirred?
When we sob aloud, the human creatures near us
    Pass by, hearing not, or answer not a word!
And *we* hear not (for the wheels in their resounding)
    Strangers speaking at the door:
Is it likely God, with angels singing round Him,
    Hears our weeping any more?

X.

'Two words, indeed, of praying we remember;
    And at midnight's hour of harm,
"Our Father," looking upward in the chamber,
    We say softly for a charm.
We know no other words, except "Our Father,"
    And we think that, in some pause of angels' song,
God may pluck them with the silence sweet to gather,
    And hold both within His right hand which is
strong.

"Our Father!" If He heard us, He would surely
    (For they call Him good and mild)
Answer, smiling down the steep world very purely,
    "Come and rest with me, my child."

XI.

'But, no!' say the children, weeping faster,
    'He is speechless as a stone;
And they tell us, of His image is the master
    Who commands us to work on.
Go to!' say the children, – 'up in Heaven,
    Dark, wheel-like, turning clouds are all we find.
Do not mock us; grief has made us unbelieving:
    We look up for God, but tears have made us blind.'
Do ye hear the children weeping and disproving,
    O my brothers, what ye preach?
For God's possible is taught by His world's loving,
    And the children doubt of each.

XII.

And well may the children weep before you!
    They are weary ere they run;
They have never seen the sunshine, nor the glory
    Which is brighter than the sun.
They know the grief of man, without its wisdom;
    They sink in the despair, without its calm;
Are slaves, without the liberty in Christdom,
    Are martyrs, by the pang without the palm:
Are worn, as if with age, yet unretrievingly
    The harvest of its memories cannot reap, –
Are orphans of the earthly love and heavenly.
    Let them weep! let them weep!

XIII.

They look up, with their pale and sunken faces,
    And their look is dread to see,
For they think you see their angels in their places,
    With eyes meant for Deity.

'How long,' they say, 'how long, O cruel nation,
  Will you stand, to move the world, on a child's
  heart, –
Stifle down with a mailed heel its palpitation,
  And tread onward to your throne amid the mart?
Our blood splashes upward, O gold-heaper,
  And your purple shows your path!
But the child's sob curseth deeper in the silence
  Than the strong man in his wrath.'

The Lady's 'Yes'

I.

'YES!' I answered you last night;
  ' No!' this morning, Sir, I say:
Colours seen by candle-light,
  Will not look the same by day.

II.

When the tabors played their best,
  Lamps above, and laughs below,
Love me sounded like a jest,
  Fit for *yes* or fit for *no*!

III.

Call me false, or call me free,
  Vow, whatever light may shine, –
No man on your face shall see
  Any grief for change on mine.

IV.

Yet the sin is on us both;
  Time to dance is not to woo;
Wooer light makes fickle troth,
  Scorn of *me* recoils on *you*.

V.

Learn to win a lady's faith
  Nobly, as the thing is high,
Bravely, as for life and death,
  With a loyal gravity.

VI.

Lead her from the festive boards,
    Point her to the starry skies;
Guard her, by your truthful words,
    Pure from courtship's flatteries.

VII.

By your truth she shall be true,
    Ever true, as wives of yore;
And her *yes*, once said to you,
    SHALL be Yes for evermore.

The Poet and the Bird

A Fable

I.

SAID a people to a poet – 'Go out from among us straightaway!
　While we are thinking earthly things, thou singest of divine:
There's a little fair brown nightingale who, sitting in the gateway,
　Makes fitter music to our ear than any song of thine!'

II.

The poet went out weeping; the nightingale ceased chanting:
　'Now, wherefore, O thou nightingale, is all thy sweetness
done?
　– 'I cannot sing my earthly things, the heavenly poet wanting,
　Whose highest harmony includes the lowest under sun.'

III.

The poet went out weeping, and died abroad, bereft there;
　The bird flew to his grave and died amid a thousand wails:
And when I last came by the place, I swear the music left there
　Was only of the poet's song, and not the nightingale's.

That Day

I.

I STAND by the river where both of us stood,
And there is but one shadow to darken the flood;
And the path leading to it, where both used to pass,
Has the step but of one, to take the dew from the grass,
                    One forlorn since that day.

II.

The flowers of the margin are many to see;
None stooped at my bidding to pluck them for me.
The bird in the alder sings loudly and long, –
My low sound of weeping disturbs not his song,
                    As thy vow did, that day.

III.

I stand by the river, I think of the vow;
Oh, calm as the place is, vow-breaker, be thou!
I leave the flower growing, the bird unreproved;
Would I trouble *thee* rather than *them*, my beloved, –
                    And my lover that day?

IV.

Go, be sure of my love, by that treason forgiven;
Of my prayers, by the blessings they win the from
      Heaven;
Of my grief – (guess the length of the sword by
      the sheath's)
By the silence of life, more pathetic than death's!
                    Go, – be clear of that day!

To Flush, My Dog

First printed in the *Athenaeum*, July 22, 1843. 'This dog,' says the author, 'was the gift of my dear and admired friend, Miss Mitford, and belongs to the beautiful race she has rendered celebrated among English and American readers. The Flushes have their laurels as well as the Cæsars, – the chief difference (at least the very head and front of it) consisting, according to my perception, in the bald head of the latter under the crown.'

I.

LOVING friend, the gift of one,
Who, her own true faith, hath run,
   Through thy lower nature,
Be my benediction said
With my hand upon thy head,
   Gentle fellow-creature!

II.

Like a lady's ringlets brown,
Flow thy silken ears adown
   Either side demurely,
Of thy silver-suited breast
Shining out from all the rest
   Of thy body purely.

III.

Darkly brown thy body is,
Till the sunshine, striking this,
   Alchemize its dulness,
When the sleek curls manifold
Flash all over into gold,
   With a burnished fulness.

IV.

Underneath my stroking hand,
Startled eyes of hazel bland
     Kindling, growing larger,
Up thou leapest with a spring,
Full of prank and curveting,
     Leaping like a charger.

V.

Leap! thy broad tail waves a light,
Leap! thy slender feet are bright,
     Canopied in fringes;
Leap! those tasselled ears of thine
Flicker strangely, fair and fine
     Down their golden inches.

VI.

Yet, my pretty sportive friend,
Little is 't to such an end
     That I praise thy rareness;
Other dogs may be thy peers
Haply in these drooping ears,
     And this glossy fairness.

VII.

But of *thee* it shall be said,
This dog watched beside a bed
     Day and night unweary,
Watched within a curtained room
Where no sunbeam brake the gloom
     Round the sick and dreary.

VIII.

Roses, gathered for a vase,
In that chamber died apace,
     Beam and breeze resigning;

This dog only, waited on,
Knowing that when light is gone
    Love remains for shining.

IX.

Other dogs in thymy dew
Tracked the hares and followed through
    Sunny moor or meadow;
This dog only, crept and crept
Next a languid cheek that slept,
    Sharing in the shadow.

X.

Other dogs of loyal cheer
Bounded at the whistle clear,
    Up the woodside hieing;
This dog only, watched in reach
Of a faintly uttered speech
    Or a louder sighing.

XI.

And if one or two quick tears
Dropped upon his glossy ears
    Or a sigh came double,
Up he sprang in eager haste,
Fawning, fondling, breathing fast,
    In a tender trouble.

XII.

And this dog was satisfied,
If a pale thin hand would glide
    Down his dewlaps sloping, –
Which he pushed his nose within,
After, – platforming his chin
    On the palm left open.

XIII.

This dog, if a friendly voice
Call him now to blyther choice
    Than such chamber-keeping,
'Come out!' praying from the door, –
Presseth backward as before,
    Up against me leaping.

XIV.

Therefore to this dog will I,
Tenderly not scornfully,
    Render praise and favour:
With my hand upon his head,
Is my benediction said
    Therefore and for ever.

XV.

And because he loves me so,
Better than his kind will do
    Often man or woman,
Give I back more love again
Than dogs often take of men,
    Leaning from my Human.

XVI.

Blessings on thee, dog of mine,
Pretty collars make thee fine,
    Sugared milk make fat thee!
Pleasures wag on in thy tail –
Hands of gentle motion fail
    Nevermore, to pat thee!

XVII.

Downy pillow take thy head,
Silken coverlid bestead,
    Sunshine help thy sleeping!

No fly 's buzzing wake thee up,
No man break thy purple cup
   Set for drinking deep in.

XVIII.

Whiskered cats arointed flee,
Sturdy stoppers keep from thee
   Cologne distillations;
Nuts lie in thy path for stones,
And thy feast-day macaroons
   Turn to daily rations!

XIX.

Mock I thee, in wishing weal? –
Tears are in my eyes to feel
   Thou art made so straightly,
Blessing needs must straighten too, –
Little canst thou joy or do,
   Thou who lovest *greatly*.

XX.

Yet be blessed to the height
Of all good and all delight
   Pervious to thy nature;
Only *loved* beyond that line,
With a love that answers thine,
   Loving fellow-creature!

From
Poems of 1850

Finite and Infinite

THE wind sounds only in opposing straits,
The sea, beside the shore; man's spirit rends
Its quiet only up against the ends
Of wants and oppositions, loves and hates,
Where, worked and worn by passionate debates,
And losing by the loss it apprehends,
The flesh rocks round and every breath it sends
Is ravelled to a sigh. All tortured states
Suppose a straitened place. Jehovah Lord,
Make room for rest, around me! out of sight
Now float me of the vexing land abhorred,
Till in deep calms of space my soul may right
Her nature, shoot large sail on lengthening cord,
And rush exultant on the Infinite.

Flush or Faunus

YOU see this dog; it was but yesterday
I mused forgetful of his presence here,
Till thought on thought drew downward tear on tear:
When from the pillow where wet-cheeked I lay,
A head hairy as Faunus thrust its way
Right sudden against my face, two golden-clear
Great eyes astonished mine, a drooping ear
Did flap me on either cheek to dry the spray!
I started fist as some Arcadian
Amazed by goatly god in twilight grove:
But as the bearded vision closelier ran
My tears off, I knew Flush, and rose above
Surprise and sadness, – thanking the true PAN
Who by low creatures leads to the heights of love.

Heaven and Earth

'And there was silence in heaven for the space of half an hour.'

First printed in *Blackwood*, May, 1847.

GOD, who with thunders and great voices kept
Beneath thy throne, and stars most silver-paced
Along the inferior gyres, and open-faced
Melodious angels round, canst intercept
Music with music, – yet, at will, has swept
All back, all back (said he in Patmos placed,)
To fill the heavens with silence of the waste
Which lasted half and hour! Lo, I who have wept
All day and night, beseech Thee by my tears,
And by that dread response of curse and groan
Men alternate across these hemispheres,
Vouchsafe us such a half-hour's hush alone,
In compensation for our stormy years:
As heaven has paused from song, let earth from moan!

Hiram Powers' 'Greek Slave'

The American Sculptor Hiram Powers and his family were among the few intimate friends of the Brownings during their first years in Florence.

THEY say Ideal beauty cannot enter
The house of anguish. On the threshhold stands
An alien Image with enshackled hands,
Called the Greek Slave! As if the artist meant her
(That passionless perfection which he lent her,
Shadowed not darkened where the sill expands)
To so confront man's crimes in different lands
With man's ideal sense. Pierce to the centre,
Art's fiery finger, and break up ere long
The serfdom of this world. Appeal, fair stone,
From God's pure heights of beauty against man's
     wrong!
Catch up in thy divine face, not alone
East griefs but west, and strike and shame the strong,
By thunders of white silence, overthrown.

Life

First printed in *Blackwood's Magazine*, May, 1847.

EACH creature holds an insular point in space;
Yet what man stirs a finger, breathes a sound,
But in all the multitudinous beings round
In all the countless worlds with time and place
For their conditions, down to the central base,
Thrill, haply, in vibration and rebound,
Life answering life across the vast profound,
In full antiphony, by a common grace?
I think this sudden joyance which illumes
A child's mouth sleeping, unaware may run
From some soul newly loosened from earth's tombs:
I think this passionate sigh, which half begun
I stifle back, may reach and stir the plumes
Of God's calm angel standing in the sun.

Love

First printed in *Blackwood's Magazine*, May, 1847.

WE cannot live, except thus mutually
We alternate, aware or unaware,
The reflex act of life: and when we bear
Our virtue outward most impulsively,
Most full of invocation, and to be
Most instantly compellant, certes there
We live most life, whoever breathes most air
And counts his dying years by sun and sea.
But when a soul, by choice and conscience, doth
Throw out her full force on another soul,
The conscience and the concentration both
Make mere life, Love. For life in perfect whole
And aim consummated, is Love in sooth,
As Nature's magnet-heat rounds pole with pole.

Mountaineer and Poet

THE simple gathered between Alp and sky,
Seeing his shadow, in that awful tryst,
Dilated to a giant's on the mist,
Esteems not his own stature larger by
The apparent image, but more patiently
Strikes his staff down beneath his clenching fist,
While the snow-mountains lift their amethyst
And sapphire crowns of splendor, far and nigh,
Into the air around him. Learn from hence
Meek morals, all ye poets that pursue
Your way still onward up to eminence!
Ye are not great because creation drew
Large revelations round your earliest sense,
Nor bright because God's glory shines for you.

The Poet

THE poet hath the child's sight in his breast
And sees all *new*. What oftenest he has viewed
He views with the first glory. Fair and good
Pall never on him, at the fairest, best,
But stand before him holy and undressed
In week-day false conventions, such as would
Drag other men from the altitude
Of primal types, too early dispossessed.
Why, God would tire of all his heavens, as soon
As thou, O godlike, childlike poet, didst
Of daily and nightly sights of sun and moon!
And therefore hath He set thee in the midst
Where men may hear thy wonder's ceaseless tune
Amd praise his world forever, as thou bidst.

The Prospect

First printed in *Blackwood's Magazine*, May, 1847.

METHINKS we do as fretful children do,
Leaning their faces on the window-pane
To sigh the glass dim with their own breath stain,
And shut the sky and landscape from their view:
And thus, alas, since God the maker drew
A mystic separation 'twixt those twain, –
The life beyond us, and our souls in pain, –
We miss the prospect which we are called unto
By grief we are fools to use. Be still and strong,
O man, my brother! Hold thy sobbing breath,
And keep thy soul's large window pure from wrong!
That so, as life's appointment issueth,
Thy vision may be clear to watch along
The sunset consummation-lights of death.

Two Sketches

There can be no violation of privacy now in identifying the originals of these two sketches as the beloved sisters of the poetess, Henrietta annd Arabella Moulton-Barrett. These sonnets appeared in *Blackwood's Magazine* during the summer of 1847.

I.

H.B.

THE shadow of her face upon the wall
May take your memory to the perfect Greek,
But when you front her, you will call the cheek
Too full, sir, for your models, if withal
That bloom it wears could leave you critical,
And that smile reaching toward the rosy streak;
For one who smiles so has no need to speak
To lead your thoughts along, as steed to stall.
A smile that turns the sunny side o' the heart
On all the world, as if herself did win
By what she lavished an open mart!
Let no man call the liberal sweetness, sin, –
For friends may whisper as they stand apart
'Methinks there's still some warmer place within.'

II.

A.B.

Her azure eyes, her lashes hold in fee;
Her fair superfluous ringlets without check
Drop after one another down her neck,
As many to each cheek as you might see
Green leaves to a wild rose; this sign outwardly,
And a like woman-covering seems to deck
Her inner nature, for she will not fleck
World's sunshine with a finger. Sympathy
Must call her Love's name! And then, I know,
She rises up and brightens as she should,
And lights her smile for comfort, and is slow
In nothing of high-hearted fortitude.
To smell this flower, come near it! Such can grow
In that sole garden where Christ's brow dropped blood.

Change Upon Change

First printed in *Blackwood's Magazine*, October, 1846.

I.

FIVE months ago the stream did flow,
    The lilies bloomed within the sedge,
And we were lingering to and fro,
Where none will track thee in this snow,
    Along the stream, beside the hedge.
Ah, Sweet, be free to love and go!
    For if I do not hear thy foot,
    The frozen river is as mute,
    The flowers have dried down to the root:
And why, since these be changed since May,
    Shouldst *thou* change less than *they*?

II.

And slow, slow as the winter snow
    The tears have drifted to mine eyes;
And my poor cheeks, five months ago
Set blushing at thy praises so,
    Put paleness on for a disguise.
Ah, Sweet, be free to praise and go!
    For if my face is turned too pale,
    It was thine oath that first did fail, –
    It was thy love proved false and frail, –
And why, since these be changed enow,
    Should *I* change less than *thou?*

A Dead Rose

First printed in *Blackwood's Magazine*, October, 1847.

I.

O ROSE, who dares to name thee?
No longer roseate now, nor soft, nor sweet;
But pale, and hard, and dry, as stubble-wheat, –
　　Kept seven years in a drawer – thy titles shame thee.

II.

The breeze that used to blow thee
Between the hedgerow thorns, and take away
An odour up the lane to last all day, –
　　If breathing now, unsweetened would forego thee.

III.

The sun that used to smite thee,
And mix his glory in thy gorgeous urn,
Till beam appeared to bloom, and flower to burn, –
　　If shining now, with not a hue would light thee.

IV.

The dew that used to wet thee,
And, white first, grow incarnadined, because
It lay upon thee where the crimson was, –
　　If dropping now, would darken where it met thee.

V.

The fly that 'lit upon thee,
To stretch the tendrils of its tiny feet,
Along thy leaf's pure edges, after heat, –
　　If 'lighting now, would coldly overrun thee.

VI.

The bee that once did suck thee,
And build thy perfumed ambers up his hive,
And swoon in thee for joy, till scarce alive, –
    If passing now, would blindly overlook thee.

VII.

The heart doth recognise thee,
Alone, alone! The heart doth smell thee sweet,
Doth view thee fair, doth judge thee most complete,
    Though seeing now those changes that disguise
    thee.

VIII.

Yes, and the heart doth owe thee
More love, dead rose! than to such roses bold
As Julia wears at dances, smiling cold: –
    Lie still upon this heart – which breaks below thee!

A Denial

I.

WE have met late – it is too late to meet,
    O friend, not more than friend!
Death's forecome shroud is tangled round my feet,
And if I step or stir, I touch the end.
      In this last jeopardy
Can I approach thee, I, who cannot move?
How shall I answer thy request for love?
      Look in my face and see.

II.

I love thee not, I dare not love thee! go
      In silence; drop my hand.
If thou seek roses, seek them where they blow
In garden-alleys, not in desert-sand.
      Can life and death agree,
That thou shouldst stoop thy song to my complaint?
I cannot love thee. If the word is faint,
      Look in my face and see.

III.

I might have loved thee in some former days.
      Oh, then, my spirits had leapt
As now they sink, at hearing thy love-praise!
Before these faded cheeks were overwept,
      Had this been asked of me,
To love thee with my whole strong heart and head, –
I should have said still ... yes, but *smiled* and said,
      'Look in my face and see!'

IV.

But now ... God sees me, God, who took my heart
      And drowned it in life's surge.
In all your wide warm earth I have no part –

A light song overcomes me like a dirge.
Could Love's great harmony
The saints keep step to when their bonds are loose,
Not weigh me down? am *I* a wife to choose?
Look in my face and see –

V.

While I behold, as plain as one who dreams,
Some woman of full worth,
Whose voice, as cadenced as a silver stream's,
Shall prove the fountain-soul which sends it forth;
One younger, more thought-free
And fair and gay, than I, thou must forget,
With brighter eyes than these . . . which are not wet . . .
Look in my face and see!

VI

So farewell thou, whom I have known too late
To let thee come so near.
Be counted happy while men call thee great,
And one beloved woman feels thee dear! –
Not I! – that cannot be.
I am lost, I am changed, – I must go farther, where
The change shall take me worse, and no one dare
Look in my face and see.

VII

Meantime I bless thee. By these thoughts of mine
I bless thee from all such!
I bless thy lamp to oil, thy cup to wine,
Thy hearth to joy, thy hand to an equal touch
Of loyal troth. For me,
I love thee not, I love thee not! – away!
Here's no more courage in my soul to say
'Look in my face and see.'

Life and Love

I.

FAST this life of mine was dying,
　　Blind already and calm as death,
Snowflakes on her bosom lying
　　Scarcely heaving with her breath.

II.

Love came by, and having known her
　　In a dream of fabled lands,
Gently stooped, and laid upon her
　　Mystic chrism of holy hands;

III.

Drew his smile across her folded
　　Eyelids as the swallow dips;
Breathed as finely as the cold did
　　Through the locking of her lips.

IV.

So, when Life looked upward, being
　　Warmed and breathed on from above,
Hat sight could she have for seeing,
　　Evermore . . . but only LOVE?

The Mask

I.

I HAVE a smiling face, she said,
    I have a jest for all I meet,
I have a garland for my head
    And all its flowers are sweet, –
And so you call me gay, she said.

II.

Grief taught to me this smile, she said,
    And Wrong did teach this jesting bold;
These flowers were plucked from garden-bed
    While a death-chime was tolled:
And what now will you say? – she said.

III.

Behind no prison-grate, she said,
    Which slurs the sunshine half a mile,
Live captives so uncomforted
    As souls behind a smile.
God's pity let us pray, she said.

IV.

I know my face is bright, she said, –
    Such brightness dying suns diffuse:
I bear upon my forehead shed
    The sign of what I lose,
The ending of my day, she said.

V.

If I dared to leave this smile, she said,
    And take a moan upon my mouth,
And tie a cypress round my head,
    And let my tears run smooth,
It were the happier way, she said.

VI.

And since that must not be, she said,
    I fain your bitter world would leave.
How calmly, calmly smile the Dead,
    Who do not, therefore, grieve!
The yea of Heaven is yea, she said.

VII.

But in your bitter world, she said,
    Face-joy's a costly mask to wear;
'T is bought with pangs long nourished,
    And round to despair:
Grief's earnest makes life's play, she said.

VIII.

Ye weep for those who weep? She said —
    Ah fools! I bid you pass them by.
Go, weep for those whose hearts have bled
    What time their eyes were dry.
Whom sadder can I say? she said.

A Man's Requirements

First printed in *Blackwood's Magazine*, October, 1846.

I.

LOVE me, Sweet, with all thou art,
    Feeling, thinking, seeing;
Love me in the lightest part,
    Love me in full being.

II.

Love me with thine open youth
    In its frank surrender;
With the vowing of thy mouth.
    With its silence tender.

III.

Love me with thine azure eyes,
    Made for earnest granting;
Taking color from the skies,
    Can Heaven's truth be wanting?

IV.

Love me with their lids, that fall
    Snow-like at first meeting;
Love me with thine heart, that all
    Neighbors then see beating.

V.

Love me with thine hand stretched out
    Freely – open-minded:
Love me with thy loitering foot, –
    Hearing one behind it..

VI.

Love me with thy voice, that turns
    Sudden faint above me;
Love me with thy blush that burns
    When I murmur *Love me!*

VII.

Love me with thy thinking soul,
    Break it to love-sighing;
Love me with thy thoughts that roll
    On through living – dying.

VIII.

Love me in thy gorgeous airs,
    When the world has crowned thee;
Love me, kneeling at thy prayers,
    With the angels round thee.

IX.

Love me pure, as musers do,
    Up the woodlands shady:
Love me gaily, fast and true,
    As a winsome lady.

X.

Through all hopes that keep us brave,
    Farther off or nigher,
Love me for the house and grave,
    And for something higher.

XI.

Thus, if thou wilt prove me, Dear,
    Woman's love no fable,
I will love thee – half a year –
    As a man is able.

A Woman's Shortcomings

First printed in *Blackwood's Magazine*, October, 1846.

I.

SHE has laughed as softly as if she sighed,
    She has counted six and over,
Of a purse well filled and a heart well tried –
    Oh, each a worthy lover!
They 'give her time;' for her soul must slip
    Where the world has set the grooving;
She will lie to none with her fair red lip:
    But love seeks truer loving.

II.

She trembles her fan in a sweetness dumb,
    As her thoughts were beyond recalling,
With a glance for *one*, and a glance for *some*,
    From her eyelids rising and falling;
Speaks common words with a blushful air,
    Hears bold words, unreproving;
But her silence says – what she never will swear –
    And love seeks better loving.

III.

Go, lady, lean to the night-guitar
    And drop a smile to the bringer;
Then smile as sweetly, when he is far,
    At the voice of an in-door singer.
Bask tenderly beneath tender eyes;
    Glance lightly, on their removing;
And join new vows to old perjuries –
    But dare not call it loving.

IV.

Unless you can think, when the song is done,
    No other is soft in the rhythm;
Unless you can feel, when left by One,
    That all men else go with him;
Unless you can know, when unpraised by his breath,
    That your beauty itself wants proving;
Unless you can swear 'For life, for death!' –
    Oh, fear to call it loving!

V.

Unless you can muse in a crowd all day
    On the absent face that fixed you;
Unless you can love, as the angels may,
    With the breadth of heaven betwixt you;
Unless you can dream that his faith is fast,
    Through behoving and unbehoving;
Unless you can *die* when the dream is past –
    Oh, never call it loving!

Question and Answer

I.

LOVE you seek for, presupposes
  Summer heat and sunny glow.
Tell me, do you find moss-roses
  Budding, blooming in the snow?
Snow might kill the rose-tree's root –
Shake it quickly from your foot,
  Lest it harm you as you go.

II.

From the ivy where it dapples
  A gray ruin, stone by stone,
Do you look for grapes or apples,
  Or for sad green leaves alone?
Pluck the leaves off, two or three –
Keep them for morality
  When you shall be safe and gone.

The Runaway Slave at Pilgrim's Point

I.

I STAND on the mark beside the shore
    Of the first white pilgrim's bended knee,
Where exile turned to ancestor,
    And God was thanked for liberty.
I have run through the night, my skin is as dark,
I bend my knee down on this mark:
    I look on the sky and the sea.

II.

O pilgrim-souls, I speak to you!
    I see you come out proud and slow
From the land of the spirits pale as dew
    And round me and round me ye go.
O pilgrims, I have gasped and run
All night long from the whips of one
    Who in your names works sin and woe!

III.

And thus I thought that I would come
    And kneel here where I knelt before,
And feel your souls around me hum
    In undertone to the ocean's roar;
And lift my black face, my black hand,
Here, in your names, to curse this land
    Ye blessed in freedom's evermore.

IV.

I am black, I am black;
    And yet God made me, they say:
But if He did so, smiling back
    He must have cast His work away
Under the feet of His white creatures,
With a look of scorn, that the dusky features
    Might be trodden again to clay.

V.

And yet He has made dark things
    To be glad and merry as light:
There's a little dark bird sits and sings,
    There's a dark stream ripples out of sight;
And the dark frogs chant in the safe morass,
And the sweetest stars are made to pass
    O'er the face of the darkest night.

VI.

But *we* who are dark, we are dark!
    Ah God, we have no stars!
About our souls in care and cark
    Our blackness shuts like prison-bars:
The poor souls crouch so far behind,
That never a comfort can they find
    By reaching through the prison-bars.

VII.

Indeed, we live beneath the sky,
    That great smooth Hand of God, stretched out
On all His children fatherly,
    To bless them from the fear and doubt,
Which would be, if, from this low place,
All opened straight up to His face
    Into the grand eternity.

VIII.

And still God's sunshine and his frost,
    They make us hot, they make us cold,
As if we were not black and lost;
    And the beasts and birds, in wood and fold,
Do fear and take us for very men:
Could the weep-poor-will or the cat of the glen
    Look into my eyes and be bold?

IX.

I am black, I am black!
    But, once, I laughed in girlish glee,
For one of my colour stood in the track
    Where the drivers drove, and looked at me,
And tender and full was the look he gave –
Could a slave look so at another slave? –
    I look at the sky and the sea.

X.

And from that hour our spirits grew
    As free as if unsold, unbought:
Oh, strong enough, since we were two
    To conquer the world, we thought.
The drivers drove us day by day;
We did not mind, we went one way,
    And no better a liberty sought.

XI.

In the sunny ground between the canes,
    He said 'I love you' as he passed;
When the shingle-roof rang sharp with the rains,
    I heard how he vowed it fast:
While others shook, he smiled in the hut
As he carved me a bowl of the cocoa-nut,
    Through the roar of the hurricanes.

XII.

I sang his name instead of a song;
    Over and over I sang his name,
Upward and downward I drew it along
    My various notes, – the same, the same!
I sang it low, that the slave-girls near
Might never guess, from aught they could hear,
    It was only a name – a name.

XIII.

I look on the sky and the sea.
    We were two to love, and two to pray:
Yes, two, O God, who cried to Thee,
    Though nothing didst Thou say!
Coldly Thou sat'st behind the sun:
And now I cry who am but one,
    Thou wilt not speak to-day.

XIV.

We were black, we were black,
    We had no claim to love and bliss,
What marvel if each went to wrack?
    They wrung my cold hands out of his,
They dragged him – where ? I crawled to touch
His blood's mark in the dust . . . not much,
    Ye pilgrim-souls, though plain as *this*!

XV.

Wrong, followed by a deeper wrong!
    Mere grief's too good for such as I:
So the white men brought the shame ere long
    To strangle the sob of my agony.
They would not leave me for my dull
Wet eyes! – it was too merciful
    To let me weep pure tears and die.

XVI.

I am black, I am black!
    I wore a child upon my breast,
An amulet that hung too slack,
    And, in my unrest, could not rest:
Thus we went moaning, child and mother,
One to another, one to another,
    Until all ended for the best.

XVII.

For hark ! I will tell you low, low,
    I am black, you see, –
And the babe who lay on my bosom so,
      Was far too white . . . too white for me;
As white as the ladies who scorned to pray
Beside me at church but yesterday;
      Though my tears had washed a place for my knee.

XVIII.

My own, own child! I could not bear
    To look in his face, it was so white.
I covered him up with a kerchief there;
    I covered his face in close and tight:
And he moaned and struggled, as well might be,
For the white child wanted his liberty –
    Ha, ha! he wanted his master-right.

XIX.

He moaned and beat with his head and feet,
    His little feet that never grew;
He struck them out, as it was meet,
    Against my heart to break it through:
I might have sung and made him mild,
But I dared not sing to the white-faced child
    The only song I knew.

XX.

I pulled the kerchief very close:
    He could not see the sun, I swear,
More, then, alive, than now he does
    From between the roots of the mango . . . where?
I know where. Close! A child and mother
Do wrong to look at one another
    When one is black and one is fair.

XXI.

Why, in that single glance I had
    Of my child's face, . . . I tell you all,
I saw a look that made me mad!
    The *master's* look, that used to fall
On my soul like his lash . . . or worse!
And so, to save it from my curse,
    I twisted it round in my shawl.

XXII.

And he moaned and trembled from foot to head,
    He shivered from head to foot;
Till, after a time, he lay instead
    Too suddenly still and mute.
I felt, beside, a stiffening cold:
I dared to lift up just a fold,
    As in lifting a leaf of the mango-fruit.

XXIII.

But *my* fruit . . . ha, ha! – there, had been
    (I laugh to think on't at this hour!)
Your fine white angels (who have seen
    Nearest the secret of God's power)
And plucked my fruit to make them wine,
And sucked the soul of that child of mine,
    As the humming-bird sucks the soul of the flower.

XXIV.

Ha, ha, for the trick of the angels white!
    They freed the white child's spirit so.
I said not a word, but, day and night
    I carried the body to and fro,
And it lay on my heart like a stone, as chill.
– The sun may shine out as much as he will:
    I am cold, though it happened a month ago.

XXV.

From the white man's house, and the black man's hut,
    I carried the little body on:
The forest's arms did round us shut,
    And silence through the trees did run:
They asked no question as I went,
They stood too high for astonishment,
      They could see God sit on His throne.

XXVI.

My little body, kerchiefed fast,
    I bore it on through the forest, on;
And when I felt it was tired at last,
    I scooped a hole beneath the moon.
Through the forest-tops the angels far,
With a white sharp finger from every star,
      Did point and mock at what was done.

XXVII.

Yet when it was all done aright, –
    Earth, 'twixt me and my baby, strewed,–
All, changed to black earth, – nothing white, –
    A dark child in the dark! – ensued
Some comfort, and my heart grew young;
I sate down smiling there and sung
      The song I learnt in my maidenhood.

XXVIII.

And thus we two were reconciled,
    The white child and black mother, thus:
For as I sang it, soft and wild,
    The same song, more melodious,
Rose from the grave whereon I sate;
It was the dead child singing that,
      To join the souls of both of us.

XXIX.

I look on the sea and the sky.
    Where the pilgrims' ships first anchored lay
The free sun rideth gloriously;
    But the pilgrim-ghosts have slid away
Through the earliest streaks of the morn:
My face is black, but it glares with a scorn
    Which they dare not meet by day.

XXX.

Ha! – in their 'stead, their hunter sons!
    Ha, ha! they are on me – they hunt in a ring!
Keep off! I brave you all at once,
    I throw off your eyes like snakes that sting!
You have killed the black eagle at nest, I think:
Did you never stand still in your triumph, and shrink
    From the stroke of her wounded wing?

XXXI.

(Man, drop that stone you dared to lift! –)
    I wish you, who stand there five abreast,
Each, for his own wife's joy and gift,
    A little corpse as safely at rest
As mine in the mangoes! Yes, but *she*
May keep live babies on her knee,
    And sing the song she liketh best.

XXXII.

I am not mad: I am black.
    I see you staring in my face –
I know you, staring, shrinking back,
    Ye are born of the Washington-race:
And this land is the free America,
And this mark on my wrist – (I prove what I say)
    Ropes tied me up here to the flogging-place.

XXXIII.

You think I shrieked then? Not a sound!
    I hung, as a gourd hangs in the sun;
I only cursed them all around
    As softly as I might have done
My very own child: from these sands
Up to the mountains, lift your hands,
    O slaves, and end what I begun!

XXXIV.

Whips, curses; these must answer those!
    For in this UNION, you have set
Two kinds of men in adverse rows,
    Each loathing each; and all forget
The seven wounds in Christ's body fair;
While HE sees gaping everywhere
    Our countless wounds that pay no debt.

XXXV.

Our wounds are different. Your white men
    Are, after all, not gods indeed,
Nor able to make Christs again
    Do good with bleeding. *We* who bleed
(Stand off!) we help not in our loss!
We are too heavy for our cross,
    And fall and crush you and your seed.

XXXVI.

I fall, I swoon! I look at the sky.
    The clouds are breaking on my brain;
I am floated along, as if I should die
    Of liberty's exquisite pain.
In the name of the white child waiting for me
In the death-dark where we may kiss and agree,
White men, I leave you all curse-free
    In my broken heart's disdain!

Sonnets from the Portuguese

I.

I THOUGHT once how Theocritus had sung
Of the sweet years, the dear and wished-for years,
Who each one in a gracious hand appears
To bear a gift for mortals, old or young:
And, as I mused it in his antique tongue,
I saw, in gradual vision through my tears,
The sweet, sad years, the melancholy years,
Those of my own life, who by turns had flung
A shadow across me. Straightway I was 'ware,
So weeping, how a mystic Shape did move
Behind me, and drew me backward by the hair:
And a voice said in mastery, while I strove,–
'Guess now who holds thee? ' – ' Death,' I said. But,
    there,
The silver answer rang, – ' Not Death, but Love.'

II.

BUT only three in all God's universe
Have heard this word thou hast said, – Himself, beside
Thee speaking, and me listening! and replied
One of us ... *that* was God, ... and laid the curse
So darkly on my eyelids, as to amerce
My sight from seeing thee, – that if I had died,
The deathweights, placed there, would have signified
Less absolute exclusion. 'Nay' is worse
From God than from all others, O my friend!
Men could not part us with their worldly jars,
Nor the seas change us, nor the tempests bend;
Our hands would touch for all the mountain-bars:
And, heaven being rolled between us at the end,
We should but vow the faster for the stars.

III.

UNLIKE are we, unlike, O princely Heart!
Unlike our uses and our destinies.
Our ministering two angels look surprise
On one another, as they strike athwart
Their wings in passing. Thou, bethink thee, art
A guest for queens to social pageantries,
With gages from a hundred brighter eyes
Than tears even can make mine, to play thy part
Of chief musician. What hast thou to do
With looking from the lattice-lights at me,
A poor, tired, wandering singer, singing through
The dark, and leaning up a cypress tree?
The chrism is on thine head, – on mine, the dew, –
And Death must dig the level where these agree.

IV.

THOU hast thy calling to some palace-floor,
Most gracious singer of high poems! where
The dancers will break footing, from the care
Of watching up thy pregnant lips for more.
And dost thou lift this house's latch too poor
For hand of thine? and canst thou think and bear
To let thy music drop here unaware
In folds of golden fulness at my door?
Look up and see the casement broken in,
The bats and owlets builders in the roof!
My cricket chirps against thy mandolin.
Hush, call no echo up in further proof
Of desolation! there 's a voice within
That weeps . . . as thou must sing . . . alone, aloof.

V.

I LIFT my heavy heart up solemnly,
As once Electra her sepulchral urn,
And, looking in thine eyes, I overturn
The ashes at thy feet. Behold and see
What a great heap of grief lay hid in me,
And how the red wild sparkles dimly burn
Through the ashen grayness. If thy foot in scorn
Could tread them out to darkness utterly,
It might be well perhaps. But if instead
Thou wait beside me for the wind to blow
The gray dust up, . . . those laurels on thine head,
O my Beloved, will not shield thee so,
That none of all the fires shall scorch and shred
The hair beneath. Stand farther off then! go.

VI.

GO from me. Yet I feel that I shall stand
Henceforward in thy shadow. Nevermore
Alone upon the threshold of my door
Of individual life, I shall command
The uses of my soul, nor lift my hand
Serenely in the sunshine as before,
Without the sense of that which I forbore –
Thy touch upon the palm. The widest land
Doom takes to part us, leaves thy heart in mine
With pulses that beat double. What I do
And what I dream include thee, as the wine
Must taste of its own grapes. And when I sue
God for myself, He hears that name of thine,
And sees within my eyes the tears of two.

VII.

THE face of all the world is changed, I think,
Since first I heard the footsteps of thy soul
Move still, oh, still, beside me, as they stole
Betwixt me and the dreadful outer brink
Of obvious death, where I, who thought to sink,
Was caught up into love, and taught the whole
Of life in a new rhythm. The cup of dole
God gave for baptism, I am fain to drink,
And praise its sweetness, Sweet, with thee anear.
The names of country, heaven, are changed away
For where thou art or shalt be, there or here;
And this . . . this lute and song . . . loved yesterday,
(The singing angels know) are only dear
Because thy name moves right in what they say.

VIII.

WHAT can I give thee back, O liberal
And princely giver, who hast brought the gold
And purple of thine heart, unstained, untold,
And laid them on the outside of the-wall
For such as I to take or leave withal,
In unexpected largesse? am I cold,
Ungrateful, that for these most manifold
High gifts, I render nothing back at all?
Not so; not cold, – but very poor instead.
Ask God who knows. For frequent tears have run
The colors from my life, and left so dead
And pale a stuff, it were not fitly done
To give the same as pillow to thy head.
Go farther! let it serve to trample on.

IX.

CAN it be right to give what I can give?
To let thee sit beneath the fall of tears
As salt as mine, and hear the sighing years
Re-sighing on my lips renunciative
Through those infrequent smiles which fail to live
For all thy adjurations? O my fears,
That this can scarce be right! We are not peers,
So to be lovers; and I own, and grieve,
That givers of such gifts as mine are, must
Be counted with the ungenerous. Out, alas!
I will not soil thy purple with my dust,
Nor breathe my poison on thy Venice-glass,
Nor give thee any love – which were unjust.
Beloved, I only love thee! let it pass.

X.

YET, love, mere love, is beautiful indeed
And worthy of acceptation. Fire is bright,
Let temple burn, or flax; an equal light
Leaps in the flame from cedar-plank or weed:
And love is fire. And when I say at need
I love thee . . . mark! . . . *I love thee* – in thy sight
I stand transfigured, glorified aright,
With conscience of the new rays that proceed
Out of my face toward thine. There's nothing low
In love, when love the lowest: meanest creatures
Who love God, God accepts while loving so.
And what I *feel*, across the inferior features
Of what I am, doth flash itself, and show
How that great work of Love enhances Nature's.

XI.

AND therefore if to love can be desert,
I am not all unworthy. Cheeks as pale
As these you see, and trembling knees that fail
To bear the burden of a heavy heart, –
This weary minstrel-life that once was girt
To climb Aornus, and can scarce avail
To pipe now 'gainst the valley nightingale
A melancholy music, – why advert
To these things? O Beloved, it is plain
I am not of thy worth nor for thy place!
And yet, because I love thee, I obtain
From that same love this vindicating grace,
To live on still in love, and yet in vain, –
To bless thee, yet renounce thee to thy face.

XII.

INDEED this very love which is my boast,
And which, when rising up from breast to brow,
Doth crown me with a ruby large enow
To draw men's eyes and prove the inner cost, —
This love even, all my worth, to the uttermost,
I should not love withal, unless that thou
Hadst set me an example, shown me how,
When first thine earnest eyes with mine were crossed,
And love called love. And thus, I cannot speak
Of love even, as a good thing of my own:
Thy soul hath snatched up mine all faint and weak,
And placed it by thee on a golden throne, —
And that I love (O soul, we must be meek!)
Is by thee only, whom I love alone.

XIII.

AND wilt thou have me fashion into speech
The love I bear thee, finding words enough,
And hold the torch out, while the winds are rough,
Between our faces, to cast light on each? –
I drop it at thy feet. I cannot teach
My hand to hold my spirit so far off
From myself – me – that I should bring thee proof
In words, of love hid in me out of reach.
Nay, let the silence of my womanhood
Commend my woman-love to thy belief, –
Seeing that I stand unwon, however wooed,
And rend the garment of my life, in brief,
By a most dauntless, voiceless fortitude,
Lest one touch of this heart convey its grief.

XIV.

IF thou must love me, let it be for nought
Except for love's sake only. Do not say
'I love her for her smile – her look – her way
Of speaking gently, – for a trick of thought
That falls in well with mine, and certes brought
A sense of pleasant ease on such a day' –
For these things in themselves, Beloved, may
Be changed, or change for thee, – and love, so wrought,
May be unwrought so. Neither love me for
Thine own dear pity's wiping my cheeks dry, –
A creature might forget to weep, who bore
Thy comfort long, and lose thy love thereby!
But love me for love's sake, that evermore
Thou mayst love on, through love's eternity.

XV.

ACCUSE me not, beseech thee, that I wear
Too calm and sad a face in front of thine;
For we two look two ways, and cannot shine
With the same sunlight on our brow and hair.
On me thou lookest with no doubting care,
As on a bee shut in a crystalline;
Since sorrow hath shut me safe in love's divine,
And to spread wing and fly in the outer air
Were most impossible failure, if I strove
To fail so. But I look on thee – on thee –
Beholding, besides love, the end of love,
Hearing oblivion beyond memory;
As one who sits and gazes from above,
Over the rivers to the bitter sea.

XVI.

AND yet, because thou overcomest so,
Because thou art more noble and like a king,
Thou canst prevail against my fears and fling
Thy purple round me, till my heart shall grow
Too close against thine heart henceforth to know
How it shook when alone. Why, conquering
May prove as lordly and complete a thing
In lifting upward, as in crushing low!
And as a vanquished soldier yields his sword
To one who lifts him from the bloody earth,
Even so, Beloved, I at last record,
Here ends my strife. If *thou* invite me forth,
I rise above abasement at the word.
Make thy love larger to enlarge my worth.

XVII.

MY poet, thou canst touch on all the notes
God set between his After and Before,
And strike up and strike off the general roar
Of the rushing worlds a melody that floats
In a serene air purely. Antidotes
Of medicated music, answering for
Mankind's forlornest uses, thou canst pour
From thence into their ears. God's will devotes
Thine to such ends, and mine to wait on thine.
How, Dearest, wilt thou have me for most use?
A hope, to sing by gladly? or a fine
Sad memory, with thy songs to interfuse?
A shade, in which to sing – of palm or pine?
A grave, on which to rest from singing? Choose.

XVIII.

I NEVER gave a lock of hair away
To a man, Dearest, except this to thee,
Which now upon my fingers thoughtfully,
I ring out to the full brown length and say
'Take it.' My day of youth went yesterday;
My hair no longer bounds to my foot's glee,
Nor plant I it from rose or myrtle-tree,
As girls do, any more: it only may
Now shade on two pale cheeks the mark of tears,
Taught drooping from the head that hangs aside
Through sorrow's trick. I thought the funeral-shears
Would take this first, but Love is justified, –
Take it thou, – finding pure, from all those years,
The kiss my mother left here when she died.

XIX.

THE soul's Rialto hath its merchandise;
I barter curl for curl upon that mart,
And from my poet's forehead to my heart
Receive this lock which outweighs argosies, –
As purply black, as erst to Pindar's eyes
The dim purpureal tresses gloomed athwart
The nine white Muse-brows. For this counterpart, . . .
The bay-crown's shade, Beloved, I surmise,
Still lingers on thy curl, it is so black!
Thus, with a fillet of smooth-kissing breath,
I tie the shadows safe from gliding back,
And lay the gift where nothing hindereth;
Here on my heart, as on thy brow, to lack
No natural heat till mine grows cold in death.

XX.

BELOVED, my Beloved, when I think
That thou wast in the world a year ago,
What time I sat alone here in the snow
And saw no footprint, heard the silence sink
No moment at thy voice, but, link by link,
Went counting all my chains as if that so
They never could fall off at any blow
Struck by thy possible hand, – why, thus I drink
Of life's great cup of wonder! Wonderful,
Never to feel thee thrill the day or night
With personal act or speech, – nor ever cull
Some prescience of thee with the blossoms white
Thou sawest growing! Atheists are as dull,
Who cannot guess God's presence out of sight.

XXI.

SAY over again, and yet once over again,
That thou dost love me. Though the word repeated
Should seem ' a cuckoo-song,' as thou dost treat it,
Remember, never to the hill or plain,
Valley and wood, without her cuckoo-strain
Comes the fresh Spring in all her green completed.
Beloved, I, amid the darkness greeted
By a doubtful spirit-voice, in that doubt's pain
Cry, ' Speak once more – thou lovest! ' Who can fear
Too many stars, though each in heaven shall roll,
Too many flowers, though each shall crown the year?
Say thou dost love me, love me, love me – toll
The silver iterance! – only minding, Dear,
To love me also in silence with thy soul.

XXII.

WHEN our two souls stand up erect and strong,
Face to face, silent, drawing nigh and nigher,
Until the lengthening wings break into fire
At either curved point, – what bitter wrong
Can the earth do to us, that we should not long
Be here contented? Think. In mounting higher,
The angels would press on us and aspire
To drop some golden orb of perfect song
Into our deep, dear silence. Let us stay
Rather on earth, Beloved, – where the unfit
Contrarious moods of men recoil away
And isolate pure spirits, and permit
A place to stand and love in for a day,
With darkness and the death-hour rounding it.

XXIII.

IS it indeed so? If I lay here dead,
Wouldst thou miss any life in losing mine?
And would the sun for thee more coldly shine
Because of grave-damps falling round my head?
I marvelled, my Beloved, when I read
Thy thought so in the letter. I am thine –
But ... so much to thee? Can I pour thy wine
While my hands tremble? Then my soul, instead
Of dreams of death, resumes life's lower range.
Then, love me, Love! look on me – breathe on me!
As brighter ladies do not count it strange,
For love, to give up acres and degree,
I yield the grave for thy sake, and exchange
My near sweet view of Heaven, for earth with thee!

XXIV.

LET the world's sharpness, like a clasping knife,
Shut in upon itself and do no harm
In this close hand of Love, now soft and warm,
And let us hear no sound of human strife
After the click of the shutting. Life to life –
I lean upon thee, Dear, without alarm,
And feel as safe as guarded by a charm
Against the stab of worldlings, who if rife
Are weak to injure. Very whitely still
The lilies of our lives may reassure
Their blossoms from their roots, accessible
Alone to heavenly dews that drop not fewer,
Growing straight, out of man's reach, on the hill.
God only, who made us rich, can make us poor.

XXV.

A HEAVY heart, Beloved, have I borne
From year to year until I saw thy face,
And sorrow after sorrow took the place
Of all those natural joys as lightly worn
As the stringed pearls, each lifted in its turn
By a beating heart at dance-time. Hopes apace
Were changed to long despairs, till God's own grace
Could scarcely lift above the world forlorn
My heavy heart. Then *thou* didst bid me bring
And let it drop adown thy calmly great
Deep being! Fast it sinketh, as a thing
Which its own nature doth precipitate,
While thine doth close above it, mediating
Betwixt the stars and the unaccomplished fate.

XXVI.

I LIVED with visions for my company
Instead of men and women, years ago,
And found them gentle mates, nor thought to know
A sweeter music than they played to me.
But soon their trailing purple was not free
Of this world's dust, their lutes did silent grow,
And I myself grew faint and blind below
Their vanishing eyes. Then THOU didst come – to be,
Beloved, what they seemed. Their shining fronts,
Their songs, their splendors (better, yet the same,
As river-water hallowed into fonts),
Met in thee, and from out thee overcame
My soul with satisfaction of all wants:
Because God's gifts put man's best dreams to shame.

XXVII.

MY own Beloved, who hast lifted me
From this drear flat of earth where I was thrown,
And, in betwixt the languid ringlets, blown
A life-breath, till the forehead hopefully
Shines out again, as all the angels see,
Before thy saving kiss! My own, my own,
Who camest to me when the world was gone,
And I who looked for only God, found thee!
I find thee; I am safe, and strong, and glad.
As one who stands in dewless asphodel
Looks backward on the tedious time he had
In the upper life, – so I, with bosom-swell,
Make witness, here, between the good and bad,
That Love, as strong as Death, retrieves as well.

XXVIII.

MY letters! all dead paper, mute and white!
And yet they seem alive and quivering
Against my tremulous hands which loose the string
And let them drop down on my knee to-night.
This said, – he wished to have me in his sight
Once, as a friend: this fixed a day in spring
To come and touch my hand ... a simple thing,
Yet I wept for it! – this, ... the paper's light ...
Said, *Dear, I love thee*; and I sank and quailed
As if God's future thundered on my past.
This said, *I am thine* – and so its ink has paled
With lying at my heart that beat too fast.
And this ... O Love, thy words have ill availed
If, what this said, I dared repeat at last!

XXIX.

I THINK of thee! – my thoughts do twine and bud
About thee, as wild vines, about a tree,
Put out broad leaves, and soon there 's nought to see
Except the straggling green which hides the wood.
Yet, O my palm-tree, be it understood
I will not have my thoughts instead of thee
Who art dearer, better! Rather, instantly
Renew thy presence; as a strong tree should,
Rustle thy boughs and set thy trunk all bare,
And let these bands of greenery which insphere thee
Drop heavily down, – burst, shattered, everywhere!
Because, in this deep joy to see and hear thee
And breathe within thy shadow a new air,
I do not think of thee – I am too near thee.

XXX.

I SEE thine image through my tears to-night,
And yet to-day I saw thee smiling. How
Refer the cause? – Beloved, is it thou
Or I, who makes me sad? The acolyte
Amid the chanted joy and thankful rite
May so fall flat, with pale insensate brow,
On the altar-stair. I hear thy voice and vow,
Perplexed, uncertain, since thou art out of sight,
As he, in his swooning ears, the choir's Amen.
Beloved, dost thou love? or did I see all
The glory as I dreamed, and fainted when
Too vehement light dilated my ideal,
For my soul's eyes? Will that light come again,
As now these tears come – falling hot and real?

XXXI.

THOU comest! all is said without a word.
I sit beneath thy looks, as children do
In the noon-sun, with souls that tremble through
Their happy eyelids from an unaverred
Yet prodigal inward joy. Behold, I erred
In that last doubt! and yet I cannot rue
The sin most, but the occasion — that we two
Should for a moment stand unministered
By a mutual presence. Ah, keep near and close,
Thou dovelike help! and, when my fears would rise,
With thy broad heart serenely interpose:
Brood down with thy divine sufficiencies
These thoughts which tremble when bereft of those,
Like callow birds left desert to the skies.

XXXII.

THE first time that the sun rose on thine oath
To love me, I looked forward to the moon
To slacken all those bonds which seemed too soon
And quickly tied to make a lasting troth.
Quick-loving hearts, I thought, may quickly loathe;
And, looking on myself, I seemed not one
For such man's love! – more like an out-of-tune
Worn viol, a good singer would be wroth
To spoil his song with, and which, snatched in haste,
Is laid down at the first ill-sounding note.
I did not wrong myself so, but I placed
A wrong on *thee*. For perfect strains may float
'Neath master-hands, from instruments defaced, –
And great souls, at one stroke, may do and doat.

XXXIII.

YES, call me by my pet-name! let me hear
The name I used to run at, when a child,
From innocent play, and leave the cowslips piled,
To glance up in some face that proved me dear
With the look of its eyes. I miss the clear
Fond voices which, being drawn and reconciled
Into the music of Heaven's undefiled,
Call me no longer. Silence on the bier,
While I call God – call God! – So let thy mouth
Be heir to those who are now exanimate.
Gather the north flowers to complete the south,
And catch the early love up in the late.
Yes, call me by that name, – and I, in truth,
With the same heart, will answer and not wait.

XXXIV.

WITH the same heart, I said, I'll answer thee
As those, when thou shalt call me by my name –
Lo, the vain promise! is the same, the same,
Perplexed and ruffled by life's strategy?
When called before, I told how hastily
I dropped my flowers or brake off from a game,
To run and answer with the smile that came
At play last moment, and went on with me
Through my obedience. When I answer now,
I drop a grave thought, break from solitude;
Yet still my heart goes to thee – ponder how –
Not as to a single good, but all my good!
Lay thy hand on it, best one, and allow
That no child's foot could run fast as this blood.

XXXV.

IF I leave all for thee, wilt thou exchange
And be all to me? Shall I never miss
Home-talk and blessing and the common kiss
That comes to each in turn, nor count it strange,
When I look up, to drop on a new range
Of walls and floors, another home than this?
Nay, wilt thou fill that place by me which is
Filled by dead eyes too tender to know change?
That 's hardest. If to conquer love, has tried,
To conquer grief, tries more, as all things prove;
For grief indeed is love and grief beside.
Alas, I have grieved so I am hard to love.
Yet love me – wilt thou? Open thine heart wide,
And fold within the wet wings of thy dove.

XXXVI.

WHEN we met first and loved, I did not build
Upon the event with marble. Could it mean
To last, a love set pendulous between
Sorrow and sorrow? Nay, I rather thrilled,
Distrusting every light that seemed to gild
The onward path, and feared to overlean
A finger even. And, though I have grown serene
And strong since then, I think that God has willed
A still renewable fear . . . O love, O troth . . .
Lest these enclasped hands should never hold,
This mutual kiss drop down between us both
As an unowned thing, once the lips being cold.
And Love, be false! if *he*, to keep one oath,
Must lose one joy, by his life's star foretold.

XXXVII

PARDON, oh, pardon, that my soul should make,
Of all that strong divineness which I know
For thine and thee, an image only so
Formed of the sand, and fit to shift and break.
It is that distant years which did not take
Thy sovranty, recoiling with a blow,
Have forced my swimming brain to undergo
Their doubt and dread, and blindly to forsake
Thy purity of likeness and distort
Thy worthiest love to a worthless counterfeit:
As if a shipwrecked Pagan, safe in port,
His guardian sea-god to commemorate,
Should set a sculptured porpoise, gills a-snort
And vibrant tail, within the temple-gate.

XXXVIII.

FIRST time he kissed me, he but only kissed
The fingers of this hand wherewith I write;
And ever since, it grew more clean and white,
Slow to world-greetings, quick with its ' Oh, list,'
When the angels speak. A ring of amethyst
I could not wear here, plainer to my sight,
Than that first kiss. The second passed in height
The first, and sought the forehead, and half missed,
Half falling on the hair. O beyond meed!
That was the chrism of love, which love's own crown,
With sanctifying sweetness, did precede.
The third upon my lips was folded down
In perfect, purple state; since when, indeed,
I have been proud and said, ' My love, my own.'

XXXIX.

BECAUSE thou hast the power and own'st the grace
To look through and behind this mask of me
(Against which years have beat thus blanchingly
With their rains), and behold my soul's true face,
The dim and weary witness of life's race, –
Because thou hast the faith and love to see,
Through that same soul's distracting lethargy,
The patient angel waiting for a place
In the new Heavens, – because nor sin nor woe,
Nor God's infliction, nor death's neighborhood,
Nor all which others viewing, turn to go,
Nor all which makes me tired of all, self-viewed, –
Nothing repels thee, . . . Dearest, teach me so
To pour out gratitude, as thou dost, good!

XL.

OH, yes! they love through all this world of ours!
I will not gainsay love, called love forsooth.
I have heard love talked in my early youth,
And since, not so long back but that the flowers
Then gathered, smell still. Mussulmans and Giaours
Throw kerchiefs at a smile, and have no ruth
For any weeping. Polypheme's white tooth
Slips on the nut if, after frequent showers,
The shell is over-smooth, – and not so much
Will turn the thing called love, aside to hate
Or else to oblivion. But thou art not such
A lover, my Beloved! thou canst wait
Through sorrow and sickness, to bring souls to touch,
And think it soon when others cry ' Too late.'

XLI.

I THANK all who have loved me in their hearts,
With thanks and love from mine. Deep thanks to all
Who paused a little near the prison-wall
To hear my music in its louder parts
Ere they went onward, each one to the mart's
Or temple's occupation, beyond call.
But thou, who, in my voice's sink and fall
When the sob took it, thy divinest Art's
Own instrument didst drop down at thy foot
To hearken what I said between my tears, . . .
Instruct me how to thank thee! Oh, to shoot
My soul's full meaning into future years,
That *they* should lend it utterance, and salute
Love that endures, from Life that disappears!

XLII.

This sonnet was not in the privately printed collection of 1847, which were 43 in all; but was first inserted when the sonnets were included among Mrs. Browning's other poems in 1856.

'My future will not copy fair my past' –
I wrote that once; and thinking at my side
My ministering life-angel justified
The word by his appealing look upcast
To the white throne of God, I turned at last,
And there, instead, saw thee, not unallied
To angels in thy soul! Then I, long tried
By natural ills, received the comfort fast,
While budding, at thy sight, my pilgrim's staff
Gave out green leaves with morning dews impearled.
I seek no copy now of life's first half:
Leave here the pages with long musing curled,
And write me new my future's epigraph,
New angel mine, unhoped for in the world!

XLIII.

HOW do I love thee? Let me count the ways.
I love thee to the depth and breadth and height
My soul can reach, when feeling out of sight
For the ends of Being and ideal Grace.
I love thee to the level of everyday's
Most quiet need, by sun and candle-light.
I love thee freely, as men strive for Right;
I love thee purely, as they turn from Praise.
I love thee with the passion put to use
In my old griefs, and with my childhood's faith.
I love thee with a love I seemed to lose
With my lost saints, – I love thee with the breath,
Smiles, tears, of all my life! – and, if God choose,
I shall but love thee better after death.

XLIV.

BELOVED, thou hast brought me many flowers
Plucked in the garden, all the summer through
And winter, and it seemed as if they grew
In this close room, nor missed the sun and showers.
So, in the like name of that love of ours,
Take back these thoughts which here unfolded too,
And which on warm and cold days I withdrew
From my heart's ground. Indeed, those beds and bowers
Be overgrown with bitter weeds and rue,
And wait thy weeding; yet here's eglantine,
Here's ivy! – take them, as I used to do
Thy flowers, and keep them where they shall not pine.
Instruct thine eyes to keep their colors true,
And tell thy soul their roots are left in mine.

From
Poems Before Congress

Christmas Gifts

I.

The Pope on Christmas Day
    Sits in St. Peter's chair;
But the peoples murmur and say
    'Our souls are sick and forlorn,
And who will show us where
    Is the stable where Christ was born?'

II.

The star is lost in the dark;
    The manger is lost in the straw,
The Christ cries faintly . . . hark! . . .
    Through bands that swaddle and strangle –
But the Pope in the chair of awe
    Looks down the great quadrangle.

III.

The Magi kneel at his foot,
    Kings of the East and West,
But, instead of the angels (mute
    Is the 'Peace on Earth' of their song),
The peoples, perplexed and opprest,
    Are sighing 'How long, how long?'

IV.

And, instead of the kine, bewilder in
    Shadow of aisle and dome,
The bear who tore up the children,
    The fox who burnt up the corn,
And the wolf who suckled at Rome
    Brothers to slay and to scorn.

Cardinals left and right of him,
　　Worshippers round and beneath,
The silver trumpets at sight of him
　　Thrill with a musical blast:
But the people say through their teeth,
　　'Trumpets? We wait for the Last!'

VI.

He sits in the place of the Lord,
　　And asks for the gifts of the time;
Gold, for the haft of a sword
　　To win back Romagna averse,
Incense to sweeten a crime,
　　And myrrh, to embitter a curse.

VII.

Then a king of the West said 'Good! –
　　I bring thee gifts of the time;
Red, for the patriot's blood,
　　Green, for the martyrs crown,
White, for the dew and the rime,
　　When the morning of God comes down.

VIII.

– O mystic tricolor bright!
　　The Pope's heart quailed like a man's;
The cardinals froze at the sight,
　　Bowing their tonsures hoary:
And the eyes in the peacock-fans
　　Winked at the alien glory.

IX.

But the peoples exclaimed in hope,
 'Now blessed be he who has brought
These gifts of the time to the Pope,
 When our souls were sick and forlorn.
– And *here* is the star we sought,
 To show us where Christ was born!'

A Curse For A Nation

I heard an angel speak last night,
 And he said 'Write!
Write a Nation's curse for me,
And send it over the Western Sea.'

I faltered, taking up the word:
 'Not so, my lord!
If curses must be, choose another
To send thy curse against my brother.

'For I am bound by gratitude,
 By love and blood,
To brothers of mine across the sea,
Who stretch out kindly hands to me.'

'Therefore,' the voice said, 'shalt thou write
 My curse to-night.
From the summits of love a curse is driven,
As lightning is from the tops of heaven.'

'Not so,' I answered. 'Evermore
 My heart is sore
For my own land's sins: for little feet
Of children bleeding along the street:

'For parked-up honors that gainsay
 The right of way:
For almsgiving through a door that is
Not open enough for two friends to kiss:

'For love of freedom which abates
 Beyond the Straits:
For patriot virtue starved to vice on
Self-praise, self-interest, and suspicion:

'For an oligarchic parliament,
    And bribes well-meant.
What curse to another land assign,
When heavy-souled for the sins of mine?'

'Therefore,' the voice said, 'shalt thou write
    My curse to-night.
Because thou hast strength to see and hate
A foul thing done *within* thy gate.'

'Not so,' I answered once again.
    'To curse, choose men.
For I, a woman, have only known
How the heart melts and the tears run down.'

'Therefore,' the voice said, 'shalt thou write
    My curse to-night.
Some women weep and curse, I say
(And no one marvels), night and day.

'And thou shalt take their part to-night,
    Weep and write.
A curse from the depths of womanhood
Is very salt, and bitter, and good.'

So thus I wrote, and mourned indeed,
    What all may read.
And thus, as was enjoined on me,
I send it over the Western Sea.

The Curse

I.

BECAUSE ye have broken your own chain
    With the strain
Of brave men climbing a Nation's height,
Yet thence bear down with brand and thong
    On souls of others, – for this wrong
      This is the curse.   Write.

Because yourselves are standing straight
    In the state
Of Freedom's foremost acolyte,
Yet keep calm footing all the time
    On writhing bond-slaves, – for this crime
      This is the curse.   Write.

Because ye prosper in God's name,
    With a claim
To honor in the old world's sight,
Yet do the fiend's work perfectly
    In strangling martyrs, – for this lie
      This is the curse.   Write.

II.

Ye shall watch while kings conspire
Round the people's smouldering fire,
    And, warm for your part,
Shall never dare – O shame!
To utter the thought into flame
    Which burns at your heart.
      This is the curse.   Write.

Ye shall watch while nations strive
With the bloodhounds, die or survive,
        Drop faint from their jaws,
Or throttle them backward to death;
And only under your breath
        Shall favor the cause.
            This is the curse.   Write.

Ye shall watch while strong men draw
The nets of feudal law
        To strangle the weak;
And, counting the sin for a sin,
Your soul shall be sadder within
        Than the word ye shall speak.
            This is the curse.   Write.

When good men are praying erect
That Christ may avenge His elect
        And deliver the earth,
The prayer in your ears, said low,
Shall sound like the tramp of a foe
        That's driving you forth.
            This is the curse.   Write.

When wise men give you their praise,
They shall praise in the heat of the phrase,
        As if carried too far.
When ye boast your own charters kept true,
Ye shall blush; for the thing which ye do
        Derides what ye are.
            This is the curse.   Write.

When fools cast taunts at your gate,
Your scorn ye shall somewhat abate
        As ye look o'er the wall;
For your conscience, tradition, and name
Explode with a deadlier blame
        Than the worst of them all.
            This is the curse.   Write.

Go, wherever ill deeds shall be done,
Go, plant your flag in the sun
    Beside the ill-doers!
And recoil from clenching the curse
Of God's witnessing Universe
    With a curse of yours.
        THIS is the curse.   Write.

A Tale of Villafranca

Told in Tuscany

First printed in the *Atheneum*, September 24, 1859.

I.

MY little son, my Florentine,
    Sit down beside my knee,
And I will tell you why the sign
    Of joy which flushed our Italy
Has faded since but yesternight;
And why your Florence of delight
    Is mourning as you see.

II.

A great man (who was crowned one day)
    Imagine a great Deed:
He shaped it out of cloud and clay,
    He touched it finely till the seed
Possessed the flower: from heart and brain
He fed it with large thoughts humane,
    To help a people's need.

III.

He brought it out into the sun –
    They blessed it to his face:
'O great pure Deed, that hast undone
    So many bad and base!
O generous Deed, heroic Deed,
Come forth, be perfected, succeed,
    Deliver by God's grace.'

IV.

Then sovereigns, statesmen, north and south,
    Rose up in wrath and fear,
And cried, protesting by one mouth,
    'What monster have we here?
A great Deed at this hour of the day?
A great just Deed – and not for pay?
    Absurd, – or insincere.'

V.

'And if sincere, the heavier blow
    In that case we shall bear,
For where's our blessed "status quo,"
    Or holy treaties, where, –
Our rights to sell a race, or buy,
Protect and pillage, occupy,
    And civilize despair?'

VI.

Some muttered that the great Deed meant
    A great pretext to sin;
And others, the pretext, so lent,
    Was heinous (to begin).
Volcanic terms of 'great' and 'just'?
Admit such tongues the flames, the crust
    Of time and law falls in.

VII.

A great Deed in this world of ours?
    Unheard of the pretence is:
It threatens plainly the great Powers;
    Is fatal in all senses.
A just Deed in the world? – call out
The rifles! be not slack about
    The national defences.

VIII.

And many murmured, 'From this source
    What red blood must be poured!'
And some rejoined, ' 'T is even worse;
    What red tape is ignored!'
All cursed the Doer for an evil
Called here, enlarging the Devil, –
    There, monkeying the Lord!

IX.

Some said it could not be explained,
    Some, could not be excused;
And others, 'Leave it unrestrained,
    Gehenna's self is loosed.'
And all cried, 'Crush it, maim it, gag it!
Set dog-toothed lies to tear it ragged,
    Truncated and traduced!'

X.

But HE stood sad before the sun
    (The peoples felt their fate).
'The world is many, – I am one;
    My great Deed was too great.
God's fruit of justice ripens slow:
Men's souls are narrow, let them grow.
    My brothers, we must wait.'

XI.

The tale is ended, child of mine,
    Turned graver at my knee.
They say your eyes, my Florentine,
    Are English: it may be.
And yet I've marked as blue a pair
Following the doves across the square
    At Venice by the sea.

XII.

Ah child! ah child! I cannot say
    A word more. You conceive
The reason now, why just to-day
    We see our Florence grieve.
Ah child, look up into the sky!
In this low world, where great Deeds die,
    What matter if we live?

From
Last Poems

The Best Thing in the World

WHAT'S the best thing in the world?
June-rose, by May-dew impearled;
Sweet south-wind that means no rain;
Truth, not cruel to a friend;
Pleasure, not in haste to end;
Beauty, not self-decked and curled
Till its pride is over-plain;
Light, that never makes you wink;
Memory, that gives you no pain;
Love, when, so, you're loved again.
What's the best thing in the world?
– Something out of it, I think.

De Profundis

It was commonly supposed, at the time of its publication, that the poem 'De Profundis' was called forth by the death of Mrs. Browning's sister Henrietta, – Mrs. Surtees Cook, – which occurred only a few months before her own. In reality it had been written not long after the tragic death by drowning at Torquay, of her brother Edward, on July 11, 1840. The difficulty which Mrs. Browning experienced, for many years, about making any allusion to that sharp calamity, which nearly cost her her own life, doubtless caused her to withhold from publication almost to the last these particularly intimate verses.

I.

THE FACE which, duly as the sun,
Rose up for me with life begun,
To mark all bright hours of the day
With hourly love, is dimmed away, –
And yet my days go on, go on.

II.

The tongue which, like a stream, could run
Smooth music from the roughest tone,
And every morning with 'Good day'
Make each day good, is hushed away, –
And yet my days go on, go on.

III.

The heart which, like a staff, was one
For mine to lean and rest upon,
The strongest on the longest day
With steadfast love, is caught away, –
And yet my days go on, go on.

IV.

And cold before my summer's done,
And deaf in Nature's tune,
And fallen too low for special fear,
And here, with hope no longer here, –
While the tears drop, my days go on.

V.

The world goes whispering to its own,
'This anguish pierces to the bone;'
And tender friends go sighing round,
'What love can ever cure this wound?'
My days go on, my days go on.

VI.

The past rolls forward on the sun
And makes all night. O dreams begun,
Not to be ended! Ended bliss,
And life that will not end in this!
My days go on, my days go on.

VII.

Breath freezes on my lips to moan:
As one alone, once not alone,
I sit and knock at Nature's door,
Heart-bare, heart-hungry, very poor,
Whose desolated days go on.

VIII.

I knock and cry, – Undone, undone!
Is there no help, no comfort, – none?
No gleaning in the wide wheat-plains
Where others drive their loaded wains?
My vacant days go on, go on.

IX.

This Nature, though the snows be down,
Thinks kindly of the bird of June:
The little red hip on the tree
Is ripe for such. What is for me
Whose days so winterly go on?

X.

No bird am I, to sing in June,
And dare not ask an equal boon.
Good nests and berries red are Nature's
To give away to better creatures, –
And yet my days go on, go on.

XI.

I ask less kindness to be done
Only to loose these pilgrim-shoon,
(Too early worn and grimed) with sweet
Cool deathly touch to these tired feet.
Till days go out which now go on.

XII.

Only to lift the turf unmown
From off the earth where it has grown,
Some cubit-space, and say 'Behold,
Creep in, poor Heart, beneath that fold,
Forgetting how the days go on.'

XIII.

What harm would that do? Green anon
The sward would quicken, overshone
By skies as blue; and crickets might
Have leave to chirp there day and night
While my new rest went on, went on.

XIV.

From garcious Nature have I won
Such liberal bounty? May I run
So, lizard-like, within her side,
And there be safe, who now am tried
By days that painfully go on.

XV.

– A Voice reproves me thereupon,
More sweet than Nature's when the drone
Of bees is sweetest, and more deep
Than when rivers overleap
The shuddering pines, and thunder on.

XVI.

God's Voice, not Nature's! Night and noon
He sits upon the great white throne
And listens for the creatures' praise.
What babble we of days and days?
The Day-spring He, whose days go on.

XVII.

He reigns above, he reigns alone;
Systems burn out and leave his throne;
Fair mists of seraphs melt and fall
Around him, changeless amid all, –
Ancient of Days, whose days go on.

XVIII.

He reigns below, He reigns alone,
And, having life in love forgone
Beneath the crown of sovran thorns,
He reigns the Jealous God. Who mourns
Or rules with him, while days go on?

XIX.

By anguish which made pale the sun,
I hear Him charge his saints that none
Among his creatures anywhere
Blaspheme against Him with despair,
However darkly days go on.

XX.

Take from my head the thorn-wreath brown!
No mortal grief deserves that crown.
O supreme Love, chief misery,
The sharp regalia are for THEE
Whose days eternally go on!

XXI.

For us, – whatever's undergone,
Thou knowest, willest what is done.
Grief may be joy misunderstood;
Only the Good discerns the good.
I trust Thee while my days go on.

XXII.

Whatever's lost, it first was won;
We will not struggle nor impugn.
Perhaps the cup was broken here,
That Heaven's new wine might show more clear.
I praise Thee while my days go on.

XXIII.

I praise Thee while my days go on;
I love Thee while my days go on:
Through dark and dearth, through fire and frost,
With emptied arms and treasure lost,
I thank Thee while my days go on.

XXIV.

And having in thy life-depth thrown
Being and suffering (which are one),
As a child drops his pebble small
Down some deep well and hears it fall
Smiling – so I. THY DAYS GO ON.

A False Step

SWEET, thou hast trod on a heart.
    Pass; there's a world full of men;
And women as fair as thou art
    Must do such things now and then.

Thou hast only stepped unaware, –
    Malice, not one can impute;
And why should a heart have been there
    In the way of a fair woman's foot?

It was not a stone that could trip,
    Nor was it a thorn that could rend:
Put up thy proud under-lip!
    'T was merely the heart of a friend.

And yet peradventure one day
    Thou, sitting alone at the glass,
Remarking the bloom gone away,
    Where the smile in its dimplement was,

And seeking around thee in vain
    From hundreds who flattered before,
Such a word as 'Oh, not in the main
    Do I hold thee less precious, but more!' . . .

Thou'lt sigh, very like, on thy part,
    'Of all I have known or can know,
I wish I had only that Heart
    I trod upon ages ago!'

The King's Gift

I.

TERESA, ah, Teresita!
Now what has the messenger brought her,
Our Garibaldi's young daughter,
    To make her stop short in her singing?
Will she not once more repeat a
Verse from that hymn of our hero's,
    Setting the souls of us ringing?
Break off the song where the tear rose?
    Ah, Teresita!

II.

A young thing, mark, is Teresa:
Her eyes have caught fire, to be sure, in
That necklace of jewels from Turin,
    Till blind their regard to us men is.
But still she remembers to raise a
Sly look to her father, and note –
    'Could she sing on as well about Venice,
Yet wear such a flame at her throat?
    Decide for Teresa.'

III.

Teresa, ah, Teresita!
His right hand has paused on her head –
'Accept it, my daughter,' he said;
    'Ay, wear it, true child of thy mother!
Then sing, till all start to their feet, a
New verse ever bolder and freer!
    King Victor's no king like another,
But verily noble as *we* are,
    Child, Teresita!

May's Love

I.

YOU love all, you say,
    Round, beneath, above me:
Find me then some way
    Better than to love me,
Me, too, dearest May!

II.

O world-kissing eyes
    Which the blue heavens melt to;
I, sad, otherwise,
    Loathe the sweet looks dealt to
All things – men and flies.

III.

You love all, you say:
    Therefore, Dear, abate me
Just for your love, I pray!
    Shut your eyes and hate me –
Only *me* – fair May!

Mother and Poet.

TURIN, AFTER NEWS FROM GAETA, 1861

The mother was Laura Savio of Turin, both poet and patriot, whose
two sons were killed at Ancona and Gaeta.

I.

DEAD! One of them shot by the sea in the east,
    And one of them shot in the west by the sea.
Dead! both my boys! When you sit at the feast
    And are wanting a great song for Italy free,
      Let none look at *me*!

II.

Yet I was a poetess only last year,
    And good at my art, for a woman, men said;
But *this* woman, *this*, who is agonized here,
    – The east sea and west sea rhyme on in her head
      For ever instead.

III.

What art can a woman be good at? Oh, vain!
    What art *is* she good at, but hurting her breast
With the milk-teeth of babes, and a smile at the pain?
    Ah boys, how you hurt! you were strong as you
    pressed,
      And I proud, by that test.

IV.

What art's for a woman? To hold on her knees
    Both darlings! to feel all their arms round her
    throat,
Cling, strangle a little! to sew by degrees
    And 'broider the long-clothes and neat little coat;
      To dream and to doat.

V.

To teach them . . . It stings there! *I* made them indeed
    Speak plain the word *country*. *I* taught them, no
    doubt,
That a country's a thing men should die for at need.
    I prated of liberty, rights, and about
        The tyrant cast out.

VI.

And when their eyes flashed . . .O my beautiful eyes!. . .
    I exulted; nay, let them go forth at the wheels
Of the guns, and denied not. But then the surprise
    When one sits quite alone! Then one weeps, then
    one kneels!
        God, how the house feels!

VII.

At first, happy news came, in gay letters moiled
    With my kisses, – of camp-life and glory, and how
They both loved me ; and, soon coming home to be
    spoiled
    In return would fan off every fly from my brow
        With their green laurel-bough.

VIII.

Then was triumph at Turin: 'Ancona was free!'
    And some one came out of the cheers in the street,
With a face pale as stone, to say something to me.
    My Guido was dead! I fell down at his feet,
        While they cheered in the street.

IX.

I bore it; friends soothed me; my grief looked sublime
   As the ransom of Italy. One boy remained
To be leant on and walked with, recalling the time
   When the first grew immortal, while both of us
   strained
      To the height he had gained.

X.

And letters still came, shorter, sadder, more strong,
   Writ now but in one hand, 'I was not to faint, –
One loved me for two – would be with me ere long :
   And *Viva l' Italia!* – he died for, our saint,
      Who forbids our complaint.'

XI.

My Nanni would add, 'he was safe, and aware
   Of a presence that turned off the balls, – was
   imprest
It was Guido himself, who knew what I could bear,
   And how 't was impossible, quite dispossessed,
      To live on for the rest.'

XII.

On which, without pause, up the telegraph line
   Swept smoothly the next news from Gaeta: – *Shot.*
Tell his mother. Ah, ah, 'his,' 'their' mother, – not
'mine,'
   No voice says '*My* mother' again to me. What!
      You think Guido forgot?

XIII.

Are souls straight so happy that, dizzy with Heaven,
    They drop earth's affections, conceive not of woe?
I think not. Themselves were too lately forgiven
    Through THAT Love and Sorrow which
    reconciled so
        The Above and Below.

XIV.

O Christ of the five wounds, who look'dst through the
dark
    To the face of Thy mother! consider, I pray,
How we common mothers stand desolate, mark,
    Whose sons, not being Christs, die with eyes
    turned away,
        And no last word to say!

XV.

Both boys dead? but that's out of nature. We all
    Have been patriots, yet each house must always
    keep one.
'T were imbecile, hewing out roads to a wall;
    And, when Italy 's made, for what end is it done
        If we have not a son?

XVI.

Ah, ah, ah! when Gaeta's taken, what then?
    When the fair wicked queen sits no more at her
    sport
Of the fire-balls of death crashing souls out of men?
    When the guns of Cavalli with final retort
        Have cut the game short?

When Venice and Rome keep their new jubilee,
    When your flag takes all heaven for its white, green,
    and red,
When you have your country from mountain to sea,
    When King Victor has Italy's crown on his head,
      (And *I* have my Dead) –

XVIII.

What then? Do not mock me. Ah, ring your bells low,
    And burn your lights faintly! My country is *there*,
Above the star pricked by the last peak of snow:
    My Italy 's THERE, with my brave civic Pair,
      To disfranchise despair!

XIX.

Forgive me. Some women bear children in strength,
    And bite back the cry of their pain in self-scorn;
But the birth-pangs of nations will wring us at length
    Into wail such as this – and we sit on forlorn
      When the man-child is born.

XX.

Dead! One of them shot by the sea in the east,
    And one of them shot in the west by the sea.
Both! both my boys! If in keeping the feast
    You want a great song for your Italy free,
      Let none look at *me*!

A Musical Instrument

First printed in the *Cornhill Magazine*, July, 1860.

I.

WHAT was he doing, the great god Pan,
    Down in the reeds by the river?
Spreading ruin and scattering ban,
Splashing and paddling with hoofs of a goat,
And breaking the golden lilies afloat
    With the dragon-fly on the river.

II.

He tore out a reed, the great god Pan,
    From the deep cool bed of the river:
The limpid water turbidly ran,
And the broken lilies a-dying lay,
And the dragon-fly had fled away,
    Ere he brought it out of the river.

III.

High on the shore sate the great god Pan,
    While turbidly flowed the river;
And hacked and hewed as a great god can,
With his hard bleak steel at the patient reed,
Till there was not a sign of a leaf indeed
    To prove it fresh from the river.

IV.

He cut it short, did the great god Pan,
    (How tall it stood in the river!)
Then drew the pith, like the heart of a man,
Steadily from the outside ring,
And notched the poor dry empty thing
    In holes, as he sate by the river.

V.

' This is the way,' laughed the great god Pan,
    (Laughed while he sate by the river!)
' The only way, since gods began
To make sweet music, they could succeed.'
Then, dropping his mouth to a hole in the reed,
    He blew in power by the river.

VI.

Sweet, sweet, sweet, O Pan!
    Piercing sweet by the river!
Blinding sweet, O great god Pan!
The sun on the hill forgot to die,
And the lilies revived, and the dragon-fly
    Came back to dream on the river.

VII.

Yet half a beast is the great god Pan,
    To laugh as he sits by the river,
Making a poet out of a man:
The true gods sigh for the cost and pain, –
For the reed which grows nevermore again
    As a reed with the reeds in the river.

My Heart and I

I.

ENOUGH! we're tired, my heart and I.
    We sit beside the headstone thus,
    And wish that name were carved for us.
The moss reprints more tenderly
    The hard types of the mason's knife,
    As heaven's sweet life renews earth's life
With which we're tired, my heart and I.

II.

You see we're tired, my heart and I.
    We dealt with books, we trusted men,
    And in our own blood drenched the pen,
As if such colours could not fly.
    We walked too straight for fortune's end,
    We loved too true to keep a friend ;
At last we're tired, my heart and I.

III.

How tired we feel, my heart and I!
    We seem of no use in the world ;
    Our fancies hang grey and uncurled
About men's eyes indifferently ;
    Our voice which thrilled you so, will let
    You sleep; our tears are only wet :
What do we here, my heart and I?

IV.

So tired, so tired, my heart and I!
   It was not thus in that old time
   When Ralph sat with me 'neath the lime
To watch the sunset from the sky.
   'Dear love, you're looking tired,' he said;
   I, smiling at him, shook my head :
'Tis now we're tired, my heart and I.

V.

So tired, so tired, my heart and I!
   Though now none takes me on his arm
   To fold me close and kiss me warm
Till each quick breath end in a sigh
   Of happy languor. Now, alone,
   We lean upon this graveyard stone,
Uncheered, unkissed, my heart and I.

VI.

Tired out we are, my heart and I.
   Suppose the world brought diadems
   To tempt us, crusted with loose gems
Of powers and pleasures? Let it try.
   We scarcely care to look at even
   A pretty child, or God's blue heaven,
We feel so tired, my heart and I.

VII.

Yet who complains? My heart and I?
   In this abundant earth no doubt
   Is little room for things worn out :
Disdain them, break them, throw them by
   And if before the days grew rough
   We once were loved, used, – well enough,
I think, we've fared, my heart and I.

Nature's Remorses

Rome 1861

I.

HER soul was bred by a throne, and fed
    From the sucking-bottle used in her race
        On starch and water (for mother's milk
Which gives larger growth instead),
    And, out of the natural liberal grace,
        Was swaddled away in violet silk.

II.

And young and kind, and royally blind,
    Forth she stepped from her palace-door
        On three-piled carpet of compliments,
Curtains of incense drawn by the wind
    In between her for evermore
        And daylight issues of events.

III.

On she drew, as a queen might do,
    To meet a Dream of Italy, –
        Of magical town and musical wave,
Where even a god, his amulet blue
    Of shining sea, in an ecstasy
        Dropt and forgot in a Nereid's cave.

IV.

Down she goes, as the soft wind blows,
    To live more smoothly than mortals can,
        To love and to reign as queen and wife,
To wear a crown that smells of a rose,
    And still with a sceptre as light as a fan,
        Beat sweet time to the song of life.

V.

What is this? As quick as a kiss
     Falls the smile from her girlish mouth!
          The lion-people has left its lair,
Roaring along her garden of bliss,
     And the fiery underworld of the South
          Scorched a way to the upper air.

VI.

And a fire-stone ran in the form of a man,
     Burningly, boundingly, fatal and fell,
          Bowling the kingdom down! Where was
          the King?
She had heard somewhat, since life began,
     Of terrors on earth and horrors in hell,
          But never, never of such a thing.

VII.

You think she dropped when her dream was stopped,
     When the blotch of Bourbon blood inlay,
          Lividly rank, her new lord's cheek?
Not so. Her high heart overtopped
     The royal part she had come to play.
          Only the men in that hour were weak.

VIII.

And twice a wife by her ravaged life,
     And twice a queen by her kingdom lost,
          She braved the shock and the countershock
Of hero and traitor, bullet and knife,
     While Italy pushed, like a vengeful ghost,
          That son of the Cursed from Gaeta's rock.

IX.

What will ye give her, who could not deliver,
    German Princesses? A laurel-wreath
        All over-scored with your signatures,
Graces, Serenities, Highnesses ever?
      Mock her not, fresh from the truth of Death,
        Conscious of dignities higher than yours.

X.

What will ye put in your casket shut,
    Ladies of Paris, in sympathy's name?
        Guizot's daughter, what have you brought her?
Withered imortelles, long ago cut
    For guilty dynasties perished in shame,
        Putrid to memory, Guizot's daughter?

XI.

Ah poor queen! so young and serene!
    What shall we do for her, now hope's done,
        Standing at Rome in these ruins old,
She too a ruin and no more a queen?
    Leave her that diadem made by the sun
        Turning her hair to an innocent gold.

XII.

Ay! bring close to her, as 't were a rose, to her,
    Yon free child from Apennine city
        Singing for Italy, – dumb in the place!
Something like solace, let us suppose, to her
    Given, in that homage of wonder and pity,
        By his pure eyes to her beautiful face.

XIII.

Nature, excluded, savagely brooded;
    Ruined all queendom and dogmas of state:
        Then, in reaction remorseful and mild,
Rescues the womanhood, nearly eluded,
    Shows her what's sweetest in womanly fate –
        Sunshine from Heaven, and the eyes of a child.

Only A Curl

I.

FRIENDS of faces unknown and a land
    Unvisited over the sea,
Who tell me how lonely you stand
With a single gold curl in the hand
    Held up to be looked at by me, –

II.

While you ask me to ponder and say
    What a father and mother can do,
With the bright fellow-locks put away
Out of reach, beyond kiss, in the clay
    Where the violets press nearer than you.

III.

Shall I speak like a poet, or run
    Into weak woman's tears for relief?
Oh, children! – I never lost one, –
Yet my arm 's round my own little son,
    And Love knows the secret of Grief.

IV.

And I feel what it must be and is,
    When God draws a new angel so
Through the house of a man up to His,
With a murmur of music, you miss,
    And a rapture of light, you forgo.

V.

How you think, staring on at the door,
　　Where the face of your angel flashed in,
That its brightness, familiar before,
Burns off from you ever the more
　　For the dark of your sorrow and sin.

VI.

'God lent him and takes him,' you sigh;
　　　– Nay, there let me break with your pain:
God 's generous in giving, say I, –
And the thing which He gives, I deny
　　That He ever can take back again.

VII.

He gives what He gives. I appeal
　　To all who bear babes – in the hour
When the veil of the body we feel
Rent round us, – while torments reveal
　　The motherhood's advent in power,

VIII.

And the babe cries! – has each of us known
　　By apocalypse (God being there
Full in nature) the child is our own,
Life of life, love of love, moan of moan,
　　Through all changes, all times, everywhere.

IX.

He's ours and for ever. Believe,
　　O father! – O mother, look back
To the first love's assurance! To give
Means with God not to tempt or deceive
　　With a cup thrust in Benjamin's sack.

X.

He gives what He gives. Be content!
    He resumes nothing given, – be sure!
God lend? Where the usurers lent
In His temple, indignant He went
    And scourged away all those impure.

XI.

He lends not ; but gives to the end,
    As He loves to the end. If it seem
That He draws back a gift, comprehend
'Tis to add to it rather, – amend,
    And finish it up to your dream, –

XII.

Or keep, – as a mother will toys
    Too costly, though given by herself,
Till the room shall be stiller from noise,
And the children more fit for such joys,
    Kept over their heads on the shelf.

XIII.

So look up, friends! you, who indeed
    Have possessed in your house a sweet piece
Of the Heaven which men strive for, must need
Be more earnest than others are, – speed
    Where they loiter, persist where they cease.

XIV.

You know how one angel smiles there.
    Then weep not. 'Tis easy for you
To be drawn by a single gold hair
Of that curl, from earth's storm and despair,
    To the safe place above us. Adieu.

Void in Law

SLEEP, little babe, on my knee,
    Sleep, for the midnight is chill,
And the moon has died out in the tree,
    And the great human world goeth ill.
Sleep, for the wicked agree:
    Sleep, let them do as they will.
        Sleep.

II.

Sleep, thou hast drawn from my breast
    The last drop of milk that was good;
And now, in a dream, suck the rest,
    Lest the real should tremble thy blood.
Suck, little lips dispossessed,
    As we kiss in the air whom we would.
        Sleep.

III.

O lips of thy father! The same,
    So like! Very deeply they swore
When he gave me his ring and his name,
    To take back, I imagined, no more!
And now is all changed like a game,
    Though the old cards are used as of yore?
        Sleep.

IV.

'Void in law,' said the Courts. Something wrong
    In the forms? Yet, 'Till death part us two,
I, James, take thee, Jessie,' was strong,
    And ONE witness competent. True
Such a marriage was worth an old song,
    Heard in Heaven though, as plain as the New.
        Sleep.

V.

Sleep, little child, his and mine!
    Her throat has the antelope curve,
And her cheek just the color and line
    Which fade not before him nor swerve:
Yet *she* has no child! – the divine
    Seal of right upon loves that deserve.
        Sleep.

VI.

My child! though the world take her part,
    Saying, 'She was the woman to choose;
He had eyes, was a man in his heart,' –
    We twain the decision refuse:
We . . . weak as I am, as thou art, . . .
    Cling on to him, never to lose.
        Sleep.

VII.

He thinks that, when done with this place,
    All's ended! He'll new-stamp the ore?
Yes, Caesar's – but not in our case.
    Let him learn we are waiting before
The grave's mouth, the heaven's gate, God's face,
    With implacable love evermore.
        Sleep.

VIII.

He's ours, though he kissed her but now,
    He's ours, though she kissed in reply:
He's ours, though himself disavow,
    And God's universe favor the lie;
Ours to claim, ours to clasp, ours below,
    Ours above . . . if we live, if we die.
      Sleep.

IX.

Ah baby, my baby, too rough
    Is my lullaby? What have I said?
Sleep! When I've wept long enough
    I shall learn to weep softly instead,
And piece with some alien stuff
    My heart to lie smooth for thy head.
      Sleep.

X.

Two souls met upon thee, my sweet;
    Two loves led thee out to the sun:
Alas, pretty hands, pretty feet,
    If the one who remains (only one)
Set her grief at thee, turned in a heat
    To thine enemy, – were it well done?
      Sleep.

XI.

May He of the manger stand near
    And love thee! And infant. He came
To his own who rejected Him here,
    But the Magi brought gifts all the same.
I hurry the cross on my Dear!
    My gifts are the griefs I declaim!
      Sleep.